THE COMPLETE BOOK OF

U.S. SPECIAL
OPERATIONS FORCES

FRED J. PUSHIES

MBI

DEDICATION

To those at the tip of the spear!

On the front cover: Two scout swimmers from the SEAL platoon egress from the ocean to survey the beach prior to the platoon coming ashore. Once the scouts ascertain it is safe, the rest of the platoon will join their teammates.

On the frontispiece: The *Delta Queen* is a method for retrieving and extracting the team. The team meets up with an MH-47E Chinook of the 160th SOAR(A). The pilot brings his aircraft to a hover, then closer and closer to the water's surface, until it rests on the water. With the rear cargo ramp lowered, the MH-47E begins to take on water. Wave after wave cascades over the ramp, and soon the flight engineers are standing in water over the tops of their boots. As the Zodiac begins to line up with the rear of the chopper, a helicopter crew member holds a red-filtered light to signal the team. The exfiltrating team aims for the ramp and the now-flooded fuselage, guns the engine, and ducks their heads. With a splash and a thud, the team is aboard. As the helicopter lifts off, all the water rushes out the rear cargo ramp, like a waterfall.

On the title page: SEALs operate in small teams and are not equipped for sustained, direct engagements against enemy forces. The nature of SEAL missions requires the platoons to carry minimum amounts of equipment, munitions, and light armament, consisting primarily of individual weapons. Although it may be considered light by SOF standards, SEALs carry more ammunition and firepower than an average conventional infantry company. Surprise and aggressiveness on target are essential to the success of Special Operations.

On the back cover, top: It may not be the fastest way in, but it is the stealthiest. A team of Force Recon Marines moves through a swamp, leaving no trace of their insertion. *Overlay:* The fast rope insertion/extraction system is the way to insert your assault force on the ground in seconds.

Edited by Amy Glaser
Layout by LeAnn Kuhlmann

Printed in Hong Kong

CONTENTS

PREFACE

When they hear the term "Special Forces," many people think of the various elite units of the United States military, including Navy SEALs, Army Rangers, and Green Berets. In fact, in the U.S. military, Special Forces refers exclusively to the U.S. Army Special Forces, traditionally known as the Green Berets. Commandos in the other services are defined as Special Operations Forces and come under the command and control of the U.S. Special Operations Command, or SOCOM. It should also be noted that although the U.S. Marines are an elite unit and are considered "Special Operations Capable," except for a special Marine Corps detachment, they are not considered Special Operations Forces and do not come under SOCOM command (see chapter 7).

According to Brigadier General Vincent Brooks, deputy director of Operations for CENTCOM, "The Special Forces call themselves quiet professionals because few people know much about what they do. The 46,000 soldiers, sailors, and airmen in the Special Forces make up less than 2 percent of the Department of Defense. Yet they averaged 280 missions a week last year [2002] in 137 countries. Special Forces include a variety of operations, from small, strategic military attacks to combating terrorism."

HYPOTHETICAL SCENARIO

Under a moonless sky, a pair of special ops Blackhawk helicopters descends into the valley below. Wearing night vision goggles, the pilots have spent the last two hours skimming the treetops to their insertion point. The lead pilot, a member of the 160th Special Operations Aviation Regiment (Airborne), checks his instruments and communicates with the team leader in the troop compartment: they are on schedule and five minutes from their designated landing zone.

The chief warrant officer, a member of the U.S. Army Special Forces, acknowledges the information and holds up a gloved hand with his fingers spread wide, signaling "five minutes" to the rest of his team. During the next few minutes, there is some shuffling around the compartment as the team of commandos makes a few final adjustments to their weapons and gear. "Two minutes," the hand now waves back and forth to the team. The CWO removes his headset and hands them to the helicopter's crew chief.

The MH-60K Blackhawk flares, and moments later it is resting on a small patch of terra firma, the rotor blades within yards of the saplings around the periphery of the landing zone. Eight Green Berets disgorge from both sides of the aircraft and immediately establish a defensive perimeter around it.

The other helicopter, an MH-60L DAP, or direct action penetrator, is performing a lethargic racetrack pattern to provide instant close air support should the landing zone be hot. Within seconds, the crew chief of the chopper on the ground confirms that all troops are out. The pilot pulls pitch, the aircraft ascends into the dark sky to join its sister helicopter, and both return to base.

As the sound of the rotor blades vanishes into the night, the Special Forces team egresses from the landing zone and melts into the surrounding jungle. Following a compass bearing, they trail the point man as they head for their target, an electrical substation five miles from the country's principal airport.

Five hundred miles away in international airspace, a MC-130H Combat Talon breaks off from the commercial airline route it has been following for the last seven hours and prepares to cross into the enemy's backyard. Equipped with forward-looking infrared (FLIR) and terrain-following/terrain-avoidance radar, the AFSOC aircrew navigates to their drop point a mile west of the airport. In the rear of the cavernous aircraft is a company of Army Rangers, equipped with the latest weaponry and state-of-the-art night-vision and infrared-laser devices.

An explosion rips though the night, turning it into day! Flames streak skyward, and billows of smoke engulf the electric substation. Five miles to the north, the airport and surrounding area go black. The pilots of the AFSOC Talon drop to 900 feet and open the side jump doors. In the vast black hole ahead of them on the ground, a series of infrared strobe lights marks the drop zone.

"Green light! Go, Go! GO!!" the crew chief shouts, as the Rangers leap out of the transport and float to the ground.

Hitting the ground and ditching his parachute, a Ranger flips down his AN/PVS-14 night-vision device and surveys the immediate area. To his right, he sees the prearranged signal. His M4A1 carbine at the ready, he pauses to observe the identification friend/foe (IFF) infrared (IR) patch of Glo tape on the shoulder of a Special Tactics Squadron sergeant.

Sign and countersign are exchanged, and a Special Tactics team emerges from the treeline. The combat controllers (see chapter 6) have been on the ground for three days, reporting data on troop movement and airport traffic. Once the substation was destroyed, they activated the infrared strobes for the incoming Talon.

The Rangers, now at the edge of the airport, race across the tarmac. One team heads for the control tower, another for the army barracks near the fence line. A third advances on the command-and-control bunker.

From the far end of the runway, a BMP-2 fighting vehicle begins firing on the Rangers with its 30mm automatic cannon and machine gun. A group of Rangers hits the ground and finds cover. The team sergeant gets on the radio and raises the combat controller at the airhead.

"Target . . . Bravo . . . Mike . . . Papa . . . Two. Engaging with 30 . . . Mike . . . Mike. Position . . . ," giving the team's controller the position and distance to the target.

The CCT sergeant instructs the Ranger to "Wait one." Out of a dark sky comes a thunderous roar, and the BMP-2 combat vehicle bursts into oblivion, the result of a high-explosives round from a 105mm howitzer accurately placed by an AC-130U Spectre gunship loitering overhead.

The CCT turns his attention to his radio on the ground frequency once again. "Ranger—clear?"

"Roger that. Driving on. Thanks."

With the last of the enemy resistance neutralized, the airport is ready to receive follow-on forces.

While the Rangers are completing their mission at the airport, across the bay a team of Navy SEALs is just beginning theirs. Swimming approximately 25 feet underwater, they head toward an enemy naval patrol craft. Using a navigation board with a compass and timepiece, one SEAL determines the path through the murky darkness, while his buddy counts kicks to determine distance.

What seems like an endless swim soon has them upon their target. A quick bob to the surface for confirmation, then back down and under the ship to place a magnetic limpet mine, which attaches to the ship with a muffled clunk. The divers set the timer and egress out to sea.

An hour later they climb aboard a Mark V SEAL craft, ready to exfiltrate (exfil) the area. While they are pulling off their LAR-V rebreathers, the enemy patrol craft has been modified with a gaping hole in its hull and is slowly settling to the silty bottom of the bay.

The skipper of the Mark V looks at his watch: 0330. Operation Moral Origins has begun. . . .

The above mission, while hypothetical, merely scratches the surface in showing the capabilities of U.S. Special Operations Forces: a combined force of specialized operators from the army (Special Forces, Rangers, and 160th Special Operations Aviation Regiment), navy (SEALs), and air force (Special Operations Wing, Special Tactics Squadron).

ACKNOWLEDGMENTS

I firstly thank God for the freedom we are favored with in this great country, and to the soldiers, sailors, airmen, and marines and their families who sacrifice so much so that we may enjoy it. May we never take it or them for granted.

I would also like to thank the following for their support: my editors, Josh Leventhal and Amy Glaser, at MBI Publishing; George Grimes (ret) and Chet Justice, SOCOM PAO, MacDill AFB; Carol Darby, Walter "Skee" Sokalski, and SSG Amanda Glenn, USASOC PAO, Fort Bragg; Monica Manganero and Tanya Johnson, PAO, Fort Benning; Ken Carter, Army PAO Pentagon; Bruce Zielsdorf, director of U.S. Army Public Affairs, New York; Kathy Vinson, Defense Visual Image Center; Lt. Cmdr Denise Shorey, Naval Special Warfare Group Two, Public Affairs Office; Capt. Kelly Frushour, USMC, Camp LeJeune Public Affairs Office; and, of course, my family.

United States
Special Operations
Command

Origins

In May 1980, the United States launched a secret raid in Iran to rescue American hostages being held in the city of Tehran. After many months of preparation, a combined force of U.S. Army Rangers, U.S. Marine pilots, and the ultra-secret Delta Force embarked on this historic mission.

What began as a gallant attempt ended in disaster, resulting in the deaths of eight of the servicemen. This debacle in the Iranian desert not only cost the lives of those killed in action, it would also cost the credibility of the United States military in general and the elite commando forces in particular.

While the causes of this disaster are many and are argued to this day, the effects of the ill-fated mission brought about a transformation in the way the American military fights wars, both conventional and covert.

The lieutenant in a SEAL platoon is responsible for the overall conduct of the mission, from the time the team boards the helicopter or other insertion vessel, to the action at target, to the time it takes to exfil the platoon safely out of the area. Along with the point man, he is the primary navigator. This officer in charge (OIC) of Alpha Platoon, SEAL Team Five, is camouflaged and ready to fade away into the desert brush.

After the failed Iranian raid, the Holloway Commission was formed to review what went wrong, what needed to be changed, and how to make those changes happen.

A few years later, the U.S. military was mobilized into action on the island of Grenada in the Caribbean, to rescue American medical students held captive by Cuban revolutionaries. Again, the elite commando units were assigned a number of tasks.

Although Operation Urgent Fury was considered successful, because the students were rescued and the insurgents were defeated, it was plagued with a multitude of inter-service problems. Communications between the services was so bad that one unit reportedly had to call the United States to get air support for its position.

The issues that arose in the mission in Grenada made it clear that while the U.S. military had an outstanding commando force and elite units, something was still lacking. This resulted in the Goldwater-Nichols Department of Defense Reorganization Act of 1986, a major overhaul of the defense structure.

Operational authority was centralized through the chairman of the Joint Chiefs of Staff. The chairman was designated the principal military advisor to the president, National Security Council, and secretary of defense. The act established the position of vice chairman of the Joint Chiefs of Staff and streamlined the operational chain of command from the president to the secretary of defense to the unified combat commanders.

The Department of Defense defines unified combat commands as follows: "Operational Control of the U.S. combat forces is assigned to the nation's Unified Combat Commands. The chain of command runs from the President to the Secretary of Defense to the Unified Commanders in Chief. Orders and other communications from the President or Secretary are transmitted through the Chairman of the Joint Chiefs of Staff. A Unified Combatant Command is composed of forces from two or more services, has a broad and continuing mission and is normally organized on a geographical basis."

The number of unified combatant commands may vary as the need arises. Currently, there are ten: U.S. European Command, U.S. Pacific Command, U.S. Southern Command, U.S. Central Command, U.S. Joint Forces Command, U.S. Special Operations Command, U.S. Space Command, U.S. Strategic Command, U.S. Transportation Command, and U.S. Northern Command (added after the September 11, 2001 attack).

The U.S. Special Operations Command (SOCOM) became responsible for all Special Operations forces in the U.S. military: Army Special Forces, Rangers, and 160th Special Operations Aviation Regiment; Air Force Special Operations Wings and Squadrons, and Navy SEALs. Although the navy placed the SEALs under this new command, the marines were not included in the original formation. However, in 2002, it was determined that the marines of Force Reconnaissance provided similar operational capabilities, and a special Marine Corps detachment, referred to as MAR-CORDET, was assigned to SOCOM.

Special Operations Forces are small units that work alone or in concert with one another in both direct and indirect military operations. Frequently using tactics of unconventional

The U.S. Army Special Forces soldier is often the eyes and the ears of a theater commander. He is a mature, physically rugged, morally straight, highly skilled, and thoroughly lethal individual who brings a new level of professionalism to an already elite military unit. As the U.S. Army Special Operations Command advances into the twenty-first century, the dynamic world of today will find the Special Forces soldier in the position of warrior, diplomat, and commando. Once shunned by conventional troops and commanders, the Special Forces today are in constant demand by U.S. ambassadors and theater combatant commanders in chief.

warfare, they are trained in the newest methods and equipped with the latest technology and weaponry. Often referred to as the "quiet professionals," the soldiers, sailors, and airmen who constitute the SOF are an elite among military forces. They are the first in and the last out. Their missions are frequently clandestine and are often politically sensitive.

In military operations other than war (MOOTW), it may be necessary to deploy a small force to stealthily accomplish missions directed from National Command Authority (NCA). Moving an airborne division or even one of the newly created interim brigade combat teams would necessitate massing aircraft and/or sealift vessels—a procedure that is anything but secret. On the other hand, placing a U.S. Army Special Forces ODA (Operational Detachment-Alpha) on an MH-47E Chinook, a SEAL team on a submarine, or a Ranger company on an MC-130E can be achieved in absolute secrecy and without drawing a lot of attention. At one time when there was a need for "saber rattling," the call went out to "Send in the marines!" Today, you don't have to send in the Special Operations Forces—most likely they are already there!

When deploying conventional forces would be too overt and diplomatic negotiations have failed, the options open to the U.S. government can be limited. Conversely, when those forces will be committed, they require the way prepared. If a rapid but low-intensity response is needed to help defuse a potentially explosive or sensitive situation, gather intelligence, or perform a surgical strike, the highly trained and capable units of the Special Operations Forces of the United States military are called in.

When terrorists flew three hijacked airplanes into the World Trade Center and the Pentagon on September 11, 2001, they awakened a great nation, and filled us with resolve. With a purpose not seen since Pearl Harbor, the nation melded together to fight a common enemy. On that day, the nation's war machine, idling at the ready, was ignited. President George W. Bush would pick up the sword of democracy with the marching orders, "Let's roll!"

The U.S. Army Ranger is a member of the premiere light infantry unit in the United States. The cornerstone of Ranger missions is direct action—more specifically, airfield seizure and raids.

A critical need arising from the ashes of Desert One was for helicopters capable of night operations. However, not only equipment, but the men to fly them would be paramount to the success of any future Special Operations mission. For such a mission, the 160th Special Operations Aviation Regiment (Airborne) was created. Heralded as "the best helicopter pilots in the world," they became known as the Night Stalkers.

Special Operations Forces Truths

The commando units of America's Special Operations Forces operate under four principles known as the "SOF Truths:"
- Humans are more important than hardware.
- Quality is better than quantity.
- Special Operations Forces cannot be mass-produced.
- Competent Special Operations Forces cannot be created after emergencies occur.

Mission

SOCOM's primary mission is to provide combat-ready forces for rapid reinforcement of the other unified combatant commands worldwide.
To carry out this mission, SOCOM:
- Develops doctrine, tactics, techniques, and procedures for all Special Operations
- Conducts specialized courses of instruction for all SOF forces
- Trains assigned forces and ensures interoperability of equipment and forces
- Monitors the preparedness of its forces assigned to other unified commands
- Develops and acquires unique SOF equipment, material, supplies, and services.

Each service and unit cross-trains in many of the same techniques, tactics, and procedures, and at times, missions overlap. However, each SOF units has a specialty in which it excels:

Service	Unit	Specialty
Army	Special Forces	Unconventional warfare
Army	Rangers	Airfield Seizure
Army	Rangers	Quick reaction/assault forces
Army	160th SOAR(A)	Covert insertion and extraction
Navy	SEALs	Waterborne activities
Air Force	SOS	Infiltration/exfiltration and close air support
Air Force	STS	Close Air Support
Air Force	STS	Combat search and rescue and air traffic control
Marines	Force Recon	Direct action/special reconnaissance

Special Operations principal missions include direct action (DA), combating terrorism (CBT), foreign internal defense (FID), unconventional warfare (UW), special reconnaissance (SR), psychological operations (PSYOP), civil affairs (CA), information operations (IO), and counterproliferation of weapons of mass destruction (CP). Special Operations Forces are organized, trained, and equipped specifically to accomplish these nine tasks.

An integral part of SOCOM is the Air Force Special Operations Command. Whether the mission calls for insertion of a SOF team, resupply, or close air support; AFSOC squadrons stand ready to answer the call, "Any Time, Any Place." A Combat Talon I is deploying flares. *Air Force Special Operations Command*

The U.S. Special Operations Forces Reference Manual defines these missions as follows:

Direct Action (DA)

Direct Action involves small-scale offensive operations principally undertaken to seize, destroy, capture, recover, or inflict damage on designated personnel or material. In the conduct of these operations, Special Operations Forces may employ raid, ambush, or direct-assault tactics; place mines and other munitions; conduct standoff attacks by fire from air, ground, or maritime platforms; provide terminal guidance for precision weapons; and conduct independent sabotage or antiship operations.

DA operations are normally limited in scope and duration and usually incorporate a planned withdrawal from the immediate objective area. SOF may conduct these missions unilaterally or in support of conventional operations. DA operations are designed to achieve specific, well-defined, and often time-sensitive results of strategic, operational, or critical tactical significance. They frequently occur beyond the reach of tactical weapon systems and selective strike capabilities of conventional forces.

Combating Terrorism (CBT)

Combating terrorism is a highly specialized, resource-intensive mission. Certain SOF units maintain a high state of readiness to conduct CBT operations and possess a full range of CBT capabilities. CBT activities include antiterrorism (AT), counterterrorism (CT), recovery of hostages or sensitive material from terrorist organizations, attack of terrorist infrastructure, and reduction of vulnerability to terrorism.

Certain Special Operations Forces, such as Combat Applications Group (CAG) or Naval Special Warfare Development Group (DEVGRU), are specifically organized, trained, equipped, and tasked to perform CT as a primary mission. Under extremely urgent circumstances, when principal National Command Authority (NCA)-designated SOF are not readily available, other SOF may perform these missions.

Foreign Internal Defense (FID)

Foreign internal defense is participation by civilian and military agencies of a government in any of the action programs taken by another government to free and protect its society from subversion, lawlessness, and insurgency. SOF's primary contribution in this interagency activity is to organize, train, advise, and assist host nation military and paramilitary forces.

The generic capabilities required for FID include skill at instruction; foreign language; area and cultural orientation; tactics; advanced medicine; rudimentary construction and engineering; basic psychological operations and civil affairs; and a wide variety of demolitions, weapons, weapon systems, and communications equipment.

Unconventional Warfare (UW)

Unconventional warfare is the military and paramilitary aspect of an insurgency or other armed resistance movement and may often become a protracted political-military activity. From the U.S. perspective, UW may be the conduct of indirect or proxy warfare against a hostile power to achieve U.S. national interests in peacetime. It may be employed when conventional military involvement is impractical or undesirable or may be a complement to conventional operations in war.

The focus of UW is primarily an existing or potential insurgent, secessionist, or other resistance movement. SOF provide advice, training, and assistance to existing indigenous resistance organizations. The intent of UW operations is to exploit a hostile power's political, military, economic, and psychological vulnerabilities by advising, assisting, and sustaining resistance forces to accomplish U.S. strategic or operational objectives.

UW includes guerrilla warfare, subversion, sabotage, intelligence activities, evasion and escape, and other low-visibility, covert, or clandestine activities. When UW is conducted independently during conflict or war, its primary focus is on political and psychological objectives. When UW operations support conventional military operations, the focus shifts to primarily military objectives.

One of the primary means of inserting Special Operations Forces is the parachute; thus, all units are airborne qualified. After attending basic airborne school at Fort Benning, selected SOF personnel receive further training in military free fall.

Special Reconnaissance (SR)

Special reconnaissance is a human intelligence function, placing U.S. or U.S.-controlled "eyes on target" in hostile, denied, or politically sensitive territory, when authorized. SOF may conduct these missions unilaterally or in support of conventional operations. SOF may use advanced reconnaissance and surveillance techniques and equipment and/or sophisticated clandestine collection methods and may employ indigenous assets.

SR may include collection and reporting of critical information about the movement of enemy forces in or adjacent to the main battle area, location and surveillance of critical or sensitive facilities in hostile or denied territory, and post-strike reconnaissance. A Special Forces soldier reports his observations using the SALUTE method: size, activity, location, unit, time, and equipment. Special Forces also include their proximity to the target.

Psychological Operations (PSYOP)

Psychological operations induce or reinforce foreign attitudes and behaviors favorable to the originator's objectives. Operations convey selected information to foreign audiences, to influence their emotions, motives, objective reasoning, and ultimately the behavior of foreign governments, organizations, groups, and individuals.

Civil Affairs (CA)

Civil affairs missions facilitate military operations and consolidate operational activities. They assist commanders in establishing, maintaining, influencing, or exploiting relations between military forces, civil authorities, and the civilian population. This may occur in a friendly, neutral, or hostile area of operation.

Information Operations (IO)

Often referred to as *cyberwarfare*, information operations involve affecting the enemy's information or information systems while defending U.S. information and information systems. Examples could be introducing a computer virus into a computer to harass an adversary or, on a larger scale, attacking main systems to cripple or destroy the nation's infrastructure—power grids, communications networks, economic centers, and so on.

Counterproliferation of Weapons of Mass Destruction (CP)

Counterproliferation refers to the actions taken to seize, destroy, render safe, capture, or recover weapons of mass destruction (WMD). SOF provide unique capabilities to monitor and support compliance with arms control treaties. If directed, SOF can conduct or support special reconnaissance and direct action missions to locate and interdict sea, land, and air shipments of dangerous materials or weapons.

TRAINING

Among other skills, Special Operations Forces are trained in any or all of the following, depending on the needs of their service (as described in subsequent chapters):

HALO and HAHO

HALO (high altitude low opening) and HAHO (high altitude high opening) parachuting techniques enable theater commanders to infiltrate SOF teams into areas that would prohibit the use of static-line parachute operations. (Static-line parachutes are round and not as controllable as the rectangular ram-air progression system (RAPS) chutes.) HALO is one of the means Special Operations Forces teams use for insertion into denied or hostile territory.

Jumpers are capable of exiting an aircraft at 25,000 feet using oxygen. They then freefall to a designated altitude, where they open their ram-air parachute system and form up together. While the maximum exit altitude is 43,000 feet above mean sea level, military freefall operations may

Armed with a Colt M4A1 assault rifle with SOPMOD upgrades, a member of the 7th Special Forces Group (Airborne) is suited up for a high altitude low opening (HALO) mission. HALO insertion allows the SF team to insert into denied enemy territory. Jumpers may exit the aircraft as high as 25,000 feet, which makes them nearly invisible to any forces on the ground.

be as low as 5,000 feet above ground level. A typical team can be deployed in a fraction of the time it would take a conventional static-line jump. Normal opening altitudes range from 3,500 feet above ground level (low) to 25,000 feet above mean sea level (high), depending on mission parameters.

SCUBA

At the U.S. Army Combat Divers School in Key West, Florida, Special Operations Forces learn to use self-contained underwater breathing apparatus (SCUBA) gear to stealthily infiltrate a target area, such as denied territory. Unlike U.S. Navy SEALs missions, most Army Special Forces missions do not take place in water. The water is merely a means of infiltration and/or transportation to the team's deployment or objective.

FRIES or SPIES

The fast-rope insertion/extraction system (FRIES), or fast-roping, is the accepted way of getting a force onto the ground expeditiously. Unlike rappelling, once the trooper hits the ground, he is free of the rope and can begin his mission.

Fast-roping begins with small woven ropes made of nylon, which are then braided into a larger rope, approximately 3 inches in diameter. The rope is rolled into a deployment bag and the end secured to the helicopter. Depending on the model of chopper, it can be just outside, on the hoist mechanism of the side door, or attached to a bracket off the back ramp.

Once the helicopter is over the insertion point, the rope is deployed, and even as it is hitting the ground, SOF members are jumping onto the line and sliding down as easily as a fireman goes down a pole. When the team is safely on the ground, the flight engineer or gunner, depending on the type of helicopter, pulls the safety pin, and the rope falls to the ground—or, in the case of a covert insertion, will be retracted into the helicopter. Such a system is extremely useful in rapid deployment of personnel; an entire SOF team can be inserted within 12 to 15 seconds.

The second part of FRIES is extraction. SEALs refer to this as SPIES, or special procedure insertion and extraction system; while the army uses the same term to refer to both insertion and extraction. Although fast-roping

While conducting a special reconnaissance mission, the SF soldier uses a ghillie suit to camouflage his position. He will report his observations using the SALUTE method: size, activity, location, unit, time, and equipment. Special Forces also include their proximity to the target. High command will determine what ordnance to use against the target and whether the SF team's position is considered Danger Close.

gets you down quickly, sometimes you have to extract just as fast. This becomes a problem if there is no place for the helicopter to land and the "bad guys" are closing in on your position. A single rope is lowered from the hovering helicopter, with rings secured to it at approximately 5-foot intervals. The rope can have as many as eight rings.

SOF soldiers wear special harnesses, similar to a parachute harness, and attach themselves to the rings by clipping a snap link at the top of the harness. Once all team members are secured, a signal is given, the helicopter takes off, and the soldiers are extracted. This allows the team to maintain covering fire from their weapons as they extract.

Once the team has been whisked out of enemy range and a landing zone can be located, the helicopter pilot brings the troops to ground again. They then disconnect from the rope and board the chopper, which completes

SOPMOD M4
Accessory Kit

Carrying Handle/Sight

ACOG Reflex
0-300m Range

ACOG 4X Scope
0-600m Range

Backup Iron Sight
0-300m Range

Visible Laser
0-300m Range

AN/PEQ-2
IR Pointer/Illuminator
0-600m Range

Rail Interface System (RIS)

QD Sound Suppressor
30 dB Reduction

Forward HandGrip

Visible Light
9 Volt

M4A1 Carbine
(5.56 mm NATO)

M203 Grenade Launcher
with QD Mount

Modified M203
Leaf Sight

Special Operations Peculiar Modification to the M4 Carbine (SOPMOD M4) Accessory Kit

Program Objective: To provide Special Operations Forces the ability to adapt the M4A1 Carbine to increase its operational effectiveness through improved target recognition, acquisition, and hit quality during day and night from Close Quarters to 500 meters.

Program Sponsors: United States Special Operations Command

Program Manager: Crane Division, Naval Surface Warfare Center

SOPMOD M4 Website: http://armo.ego.crane.navy.mil/408html/sopmod3.htm

The M4A1 carbine is a most capable and deadly weapon suitable to any SOF mission. USASOC wanted to make the weapon even more effective, whether for close engagements or long-range targets. To accomplish this, USSOCOM and Crane Division, Naval Surface Warfare Center, developed the SOPMOD kit, introduced in 1994. *Department of Defense*

the extraction. (Although the helicopter has a hoist, it will carry only one person at a time, the person must hold on, and his extraction is limited to the speed of the winch. SPIES allows eight troops to be attached, their hands free to fire their weapons, and they can lift off the ground at the speed of the helicopter.)

WEAPONS AND EQUIPMENT

Special Operations Peculiar Modification (SOPMOD) M4A1 Carbine

As a basic-issue weapon for a Special Operations soldier, the M4A1 was chosen for its accuracy, range, availability of ammunition, ease of maintenance, and penetrating power. The M4A1 has a rifling twist of one in 7 inches, making it compatible with the full range of 5.56mm ammunition. Selective-fire controls have eliminated the three-round burst, replacing it with safe, semiautomatic, and full automatic fire.

The carbine's sighting system contains dual apertures, one allowing for 0 to 200 meters and a smaller opening for targets at 500 to 600 meters. In Operation Desert Storm, certain elements were equipped with suppressed 9mm rifles while performing special reconnaissance missions. When one of the teams was compromised and faced a rush of oncoming Iraqi soldiers and local nomads, the M16 and carbines laid down a hail of 5.56mm rounds out to 600 meters, allowing the team the extra edge they needed to extract from a bad situation. The same was true in Somalia, where the M16 Carbine proved to be more durable, versatile, and the 5.56mm ammunition more lethal than the 9mm pistol round.

M4A1 Carbine Specifications

Caliber: 5.56mm
Weight: (Without magazine) 5.9 pounds;
(with loaded magazine, 30 rounds) 6.9 pounds
Length: (Stock extended) 33.0 inches; (stock retracted) 29.8 inches
Barrel length: 14.5 inches
Muzzle velocity: 2,900 feet per second
Muzzle energy: 1,213 foot-pounds
Maximum effective range: 600 meters
Cyclic rate of fire: 700 to 950 rounds per minute
Fire selection: Semiautomatic/full automatic

Special Operations Pecular Modification (SOPMOD) M4A1 Accessory Kit

The SOPMOD accessory kit consists of numerous components that can be attached directly on the M4A1 carbine or to the rail interface system (RIS). These accessories give the operator the flexibility to choose the appropriate optics, lasers, lights, and so on, depending on mission parameters. The SOPMOD kit is constantly being evaluated, and research is ongoing to further enhance the M4A1's operability, functionality, and lethality. Components include:

M4A1 rail interface system (RIS). The rail interface system (RIS) is a notched rail system that replaces the front handguards on the M4A1 receiver. Located on the top, bottom, and sides of the barrel, this rail system, facilitates attaching SOPMOD kit components on any of the four sides.

M4A1 forward handgrip. The forward or vertical handgrip attaches to the bottom of the RIS and provides added support, giving the operator a more stable firing platform. It can be used as a monopod in a supported position and allows the operator to hold the weapon despite overheating. The forward handgrip can be used to push against the assault sling and stabilize the weapon with isometric tension during close-quarter battle/close-range engagement.

Quick attach suppressor. The quick attach/detach sound suppressor kit Mark 4 Mod 0 (QAD suppressor) can quickly be placed on or removed from the M4A1 carbine. With the suppressor in place, the weapon's report is reduced by a minimum of 28 decibels. The 5.56mm round is supersonic, so you will hear the bang, but it is more like a .22-caliber pistol than a 5.56mm round.

M4A1 advance combat optical gunsight (ACOG). The ACOG is a four-power telescopic sight that includes a ballistic compensating reticle. This reticle provides increase capability to direct, identify, and hit targets to the M4A1's maximum effective range.

Aimpoint Comp-M. Although not an official part of the SOPMOD kit, the Aimpoint Comp-M is used for close-quarter battle activities. After extensive testing, the U.S. Army adopted the Aimpoint Comp-M as its red-dot sighting system.

Holographic display sight (HDS). The HDS displays a holographic reticle pattern designed for instant target acquisition under any lighting situations without covering or obscuring the point of aim. The holographic reticle can be seen through the sight, providing the operator with a large view of the target or zone of engagement. Unlike other optics, the HDS is passive and gives off no telltale signature. The hallmarks of the HDS are speed and ease of use, providing incredible accuracy and instant sight-on-target operation, which can be the difference between life and death in close-quarter battle.

AN/PEQ-2 infrared illuminator/aiming laser. The AN/PEQ-2 infrared target pointer/illuminator/aiming laser (ITPIAL) allows the M4A1 to be effectively employed to 300 meters with standard-issue night-vision goggles (NVG) or a weapon-mounted night-vision device, such as an AN/PVS-14.

AN/PVS-14 Nigh-Vision Device

The AN/PVS-14D is the optimum night-vision monocular ensemble for special applications. The monocular or pocket-scope can be handheld or mounted on a facemask, helmet, or weapon.

MP5 Submachine Gun

Although the M4A1 is the standard weapon for U.S. Special Operations Forces, the MP5 submachine gun can still be found in the armory of these elite units. Developed by HK especially for the U.S. Navy SEALs, the MP5 "Navy" model comes standard with an ambidextrous trigger group and threaded barrel. The MP5-N fires from a closed and locked bolt in either the semiautomatic or automatic mode.

This sub-gun is recoil operated and has a unique delayed-roller locked-bolt system, a retractable butt stock, a removable suppressor, and an illuminating flashlight integral to the forward hand guard. The flashlight is operated by a pressure switch custom-fitted to the pistol grip. The basic configuration of this weapon makes for an ideal size, weight, and close-quarter-battle-capable weapon system.

M249 Squad Automatic Weapon

The 5.56mm M249 squad automatic weapon forms the basis of firepower for the fire team. It is an individually portable, magazine- or disintegrating-metallic-link-belt-fed light machine gun, with fixed headspace and a quick-change barrel. The air-cooled, gas-operated SAW fires from the open-bolt position. It has a regulator for selecting either normal (750 rounds per minute) or maximum (1,000 rounds per minute) rate of fire.

The M249 engages point targets out to 800 meters, firing the improved NATO standard 5.56mm cartridge. The gunner has the option of using 30-round M16 magazines or linked ammunition from preloaded 200-round plastic magazines and will carry a basic load of 600 rounds. The paratrooper or SOF version of the M249 has a retractable stock instead of a fixed stock and is referred to as the Para-SAW. It is also fitted with the rail system for attaching optics, laser, and other devices.

Proficiency with SCUBA gear is another skill in the SOF kit bag. Army and Air Force units mostly use SCUBA as a means of infil or exfil. SEALs get extensive practice in these procedures, because they must often be in or under the water to accomplish their missions as well as to perform insertions and extractions.

M240 Medium Machine Gun

The U.S. Army uses the M240B medium machine gun, while the U.S. Marines have chosen the M240G as a replacement for the M60 family of machine guns. Manufactured by Fabrique Nationale, the 24.2-pound M240 medium machine gun is a gas-operated, air-cooled, link-belt-fed weapon that fires the 7.62 x 51mm round. It fires from an open-bolt position with a maximum effective range of 1,100 meters. The rate of fire is adjustable from 750–1,400 rounds per minute through an adjustable gas regulator.

The M240 features a folding bipod that attaches to the receiver, a quick-change barrel assembly, a feed cover and bolt assembly that enables closure of the cover regardless of bolt position, a plastic butt-stock, and an integral optical sight rail. While it possesses many of the same characteristics of the older M60, it is more durable, reliable, and maintainable.

M60E3 Machine Gun

Still popular with the Navy SEALs is the M60E3 7.62mm machine gun. This modified version of the M60 is a lightweight, air-cooled, disintegrating-metallic-link-belt-fed portable machine gun. It is gas operated, with fixed headspace and timing, which permits rapid changing of barrels.

Like its predecessor, the M60, it is designed for ground operations, but it differs slightly in having a receiver-attached bipod, which easily deploys for stability. It has an ambidextrous safety, universal sling attachments, a carrying handle on the barrel, and a simplified gas system. While the original M60 was a crew-served weapon, Navy SEALs consider this

M240B Specifications

Manufacturer: Fabrique Nationale Manufacturing, Inc.
Length: 47.5 inches
Weight: 24.2 pounds
Bore diameter: 7.62mm
Rates of fire: Cyclic; 650 to 950 rounds per minute

an individual weapon. It is not uncommon for the weapon to deliver accurate fire from a shoulder-mounted stance.

M82A1 Semiautomatic Rifle

When the mission calls for hard target interdiction (HTI) at long range—over 1,000 meters—SOF teams turn to the big guns. HTI will take out targets such as a generator or an airplane, helicopter, or other vehicle. The M82A1 is a one-man, portable, air-cooled, semiautomatic rifle with a magazine holding up to 10 rounds of .50-caliber Browning machine-gun ammunition. Other features include a quick-detachable bipod with spiked feet, iron sights, and an M1913 (Picatinny) optical rail to accommodate various sighting and aiming devices.

AT4 Antitank Weapon

The M136 AT4 is the Army's principal light antitank weapon, providing precision delivery of an 84mm high-explosive warhead, with negligible recoil. This man-portable, self-contained, anti-armor weapon consists of a free-flight, fin-stabilized, rocket-type cartridge packed in an expendable, one-piece, fiberglass-wrapped tube. Unlike the M72 light anti-tank weapon, the AT4 launcher does not need to be extended before firing.

When the warhead makes impact with the target, the nosecone crushes, and the impact sensor activates the internal fuse. Upon ignition, the piezoelectric fuse element triggers the detonator, initiating the main charge. This results in penetration when the main charge fires, sending the warhead body into a directional gas jet capable of penetrating over 17 inches of armor plate. The aftereffects are "spalling"—fragmentation and explosions generating blinding light and obliterating the interior of the target.

The fast rope insertion/extraction system is the way to insert your assault force on the ground in seconds.

M203 Grenade Launcher

The quick attach/detach M203 mount and leaf sight, when combined with the standard M203 grenade launcher, provides additional firepower to the operator, giving both point and area engagement capability. The quick-attach M203 combines flexibility and lethality in one weapon. This grenade has a deadly radius of 5 meters.

M224 Mortar

The M224 60mm lightweight company mortar system (LWCMS) is ideally suited to Ranger operations. It can be drop-fired (conventional mode) or trigger-fired (conventional or handheld mode).

M18A1 Mine

More commonly referred to as the Claymore mine, the M18A1 is primarily employed as a defensive weapon, although it has been known to be employed in certain situations as an offensive weapon. It can be deployed as a mine, an offensive weapon, or a booby trap; it also has uses as a pursuit-deterrence device. It can be sighted directionally to provide fragmentation over a specific target area and can be command detonated.

The M18A1 antipersonnel mine is a curved rectangular plastic case that contains a layer of composition C3 explosive. Packed in the explosive are 700 steel balls. The front face containing the steel balls is

Although fast-roping gets you down quickly, sometimes you have to extract just as fast.

A SOTIC sniper is qualified to shoot at "close proximity" of U.S. troops and noncombatants. In simple terms, this means he can drop an enemy standing right next to you.

designed to produce an arc-shaped spray, which can be aimed at a predetermined target area. It comes in a bandolier, which includes the M18A1 mine, an M57 firing device, M40 test set, and an electrical blasting cap assembly.

M112 Block Demolition Charge

The M112 consists of 1.25 pounds of composition C4 packed in an olive-drab Mylar-film container with pressure-sensitive adhesive tape on one surface. A peelable paper cover protects the tape. Composition C4 is white with a unique lemon smell. M112 block charge is used in all types of demolition work, primarily for cutting and breaching. Because of its moldability, the charge is appropriate for cutting irregularly shaped targets, such as steel, steel beams, and so on. The adhesive backing allows the charge to be attached to any relatively flat, clean, dry surface in above freezing temperatures.

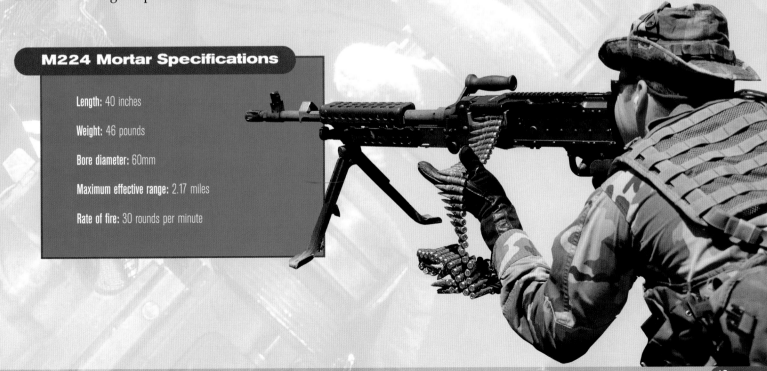

M224 Mortar Specifications

Length: 40 inches

Weight: 46 pounds

Bore diameter: 60mm

Maximum effective range: 2.17 miles

Rate of fire: 30 rounds per minute

CHAPTER 2

U.S. Navy SEALs

Motto: The Only Easy Day Was Yesterday

SEALs are a naval multiuse combat force trained, organized, and equipped to plan, conduct, and support an assortment of special missions in all operational environments. SEALs operate in small units called platoons. The SEAL platoon is the largest operational element that will normally be employed to conduct a tactical mission.

SEAL is an acronym for SEa, Air, and Land. SEALs are qualified in diving and parachuting and are experts at combat swimming, navigation, demolitions, weapons, and many other skills. In addition to the maritime environment, SEALs train in the desert, in the jungle, in cold weather, and in urban surroundings.

A Navy SEAL braves the surf as he transitions from the ocean to the shoreline. He keeps the mouthpiece of his LAR-V rebreather in place in case he is engaged by the enemy and must evade back into the water.

HISTORY

SEAL teams trace their history to the first group of volunteers selected from the Naval Construction Battalions in the spring of 1943. Their mission was to clear obstacles from beaches chosen for amphibious landings, which began the first formal training of the naval combat demolition units (NCDUs). The NCDUs distinguished themselves at Utah and Omaha Beaches in Normandy as well as in Southern France. In the Pacific, the NCDUs were consolidated into underwater demolition teams (UDTs).

The newly formed UDTs saw action in every corner of the Pacific during World War II. Beginning in 1950, they were active in the Korean War, participating at Inchon, Wonsan, Iwon, and Chinnampo. The redeployment of United Nations Forces featured the UDTs conducting delaying operations using guerrilla warfare. These navy commandos would lay the groundwork for future SEAL operations.

In January 1962, the first SEAL teams were commissioned to conduct unconventional warfare, counterguerrilla warfare, and clandestine operations in maritime and riverine environments. These teams were SEAL Team One on the West Coast and SEAL Team Two on the East Coast. In Vietnam, the SEALs compiled an impressive record of combat successes.

Since the close of the Vietnam conflict, the ever-changing world situation and increased operational tasking have prompted the expansion of SEAL teams in numbers, size, and capabilities. To effectively respond to this evolutionary process, underwater demolition teams have been redesignated SEAL or SEAL delivery vehicle (SDV) teams (explained later in this chapter). The newly designated SEAL teams acquired the SEAL mission and retained the amphibious support mission inherited from their UDT forefathers.

STRUCTURE

A SEAL platoon consists of 16 SEALs, normally commanded by a navy lieutenant (O-3). A platoon may be divided into two squads or four elements. All SEAL platoon personnel are dive, parachute, and demolitions qualified.

SEAL platoons conduct direct action, unconventional warfare, foreign internal defense, special reconnaissance, and counterterrorist operations, primarily in the maritime and riverine environments. These operations include sabotage, demolition, intelligence collection, hydrographic reconnaissance, and training and advising friendly military forces in the conduct of naval and joint Special Operations.

A SEAL squad patrols up from the beach, weapons at the ready, their attention alert to any enemy activity. Such an insertion would normally be conducted under cover of darkness.

SEAL platoons can destroy or sabotage enemy shipping, port and harbor facilities, bridges, railway lines, communications centers, and other lines of communication in and around maritime and riverine environments. They can infiltrate and exfiltrate selected personnel by submarine, surface vessel, aircraft, or land vehicle. They can conduct reconnaissance and surveillance in multiple environments, as well as other intelligence-gathering tasks, including capture of key personnel. They can organize, train, and assist U.S., allied, and other friendly military or paramilitary forces in the conduct of Special Operations.

On a limited scale, SEALs are involved in civil-action tasks normally associated with foreign internal-defense and humanitarian-assistance operations, such as medical aid, elementary civil engineering activities, and boat operations and maintenance for the indigenous population. They can also integrate naval special warfare (NSW) task organizations into fleet task forces or groups to plan, coordinate, and conduct maritime Special Operations. These may

Two scout swimmers from the SEAL platoon egress from the ocean to survey the beach prior to the platoon coming ashore. Once the scouts ascertain it is safe, the rest of the platoon will join their teammates.

include hydrographic reconnaissance and obstacle clearance; visit, board, search and seizure; initial terminal guidance; and combat swimmer operations. SEAL teams may be employed in direct support of conventional naval and maritime operations.

East Coast SEAL teams have even numbers: ST-2, ST-4, ST-8, and ST-10. (ST-6, which specializes in counter-terrorist operations, was redesignated DEVGRU, and ST-6 was deactivated.) West Coast teams have odd numbers: ST-1, ST-3, ST-5, and ST-7.

A SEAL provides security while the rest of his squad comes ashore.

Once past the surf zone, he removes his swim fins and proceeds across the beach.

Mission accomplished, the SEALs will now exit to the sea in this Zodiac raft. Like Special Operations missions, the sea is unforgiving, so SEALs train as they will fight. SEALs are at home in the water—for them it is safety and survival.

SEAL Delivery Vehicle Teams

The SEAL delivery vehicle (SDV) task unit is an operational element employed to carry out submersible system operations from specially configured submarines equipped with dry deck shelters (DDS). This is a dry launch area attached to a submarine that allows SEALs to prepare their equipment or SDV teams to prepare SDVs for launch. The compartment is then flooded and opened to the sea for launch. They also conduct specialized missions using the dry deck shelter/host submarine as an insertion/extraction platform.

Member of a SEAL team fast-rope from a 20th Special Operations Squadron MH-53J Pave Low III helicopter to the bridge of the vehicle cargo ship *Cape Mohican* during the joint service exercise Ocean Venture '92. The SEALs are practicing shipboard insertion and exfiltration techniques, which may later be used for actual visit, board, search and seizure missions. *Defense Visual Information Center*

Capabilities of SDV teams include: limited direct-action missions, such as port and harbor anti-shipping attacks and raids; hydrographic reconnaissance and other intelligence-gathering missions; infiltration, exfiltration, and resupply. SDV personnel maintain limited capabilities to operate in riverine and maritime environments, in either desert, arctic, or jungle climates.

Each SDV team is organized into a logistic support element, four SDV platoons, and two DDS platoons. The SDV task unit is normally commanded by an SDV team commanding officer or executive officer and consists of one or more SDV or SEAL platoons. When embarked in a submarine with dry deck shelters attached, the platoon commander reports to the submarine commanding officer as a department head and does not fall under the operational control of the SDV task unit commander.

SDV unit capabilities include limited direct-action missions, such as port and harbor anti-shipping attacks and raids. Special mission units, using the SEAL delivery vehicle from the dry deck shelter, or the dry deck shelter alone, can conduct a variety of direct action missions in the maritime environment. SDV task units conduct

Members of SEAL Delivery Vehicle Team Two approach the shoreline after inserting from a Mark V Special Operations craft, seen in the background. The team will approach on a skirmish line to afford them the greatest amount of firepower should they encounter the enemy. Once on the beach, they will establish a predetermined formation and proceed inland to carry out their mission.

This is an SDV squad—note the sniper in ghillie suit (used for camouflage) in the back row.

Options available to an SDV team commander to meet different tactical situations include launch and recovery via submarine or via surface combatant or noncombatant craft. The most clandestine option is submarine launch and recovery.

This platoon leader of an SDV team is armed with the M4A1 carbine with M203 40mm grenade launcher. He is also carrying a radio, ammunition, a knife, and other mission-essential gear.

hydrographic reconnaissance and other intelligence-gathering missions and infiltrate, exfiltrate, and resupply Special Operations Forces.

Special Boat Teams

Special Boat Teams (SBTs) operate a variety of Special Operations surface craft in both the maritime and riverine environments. Their unique capabilities in the littoral battle space include the ability to transition from the blue-water open ocean to beach landing sites, to operations within inland maritime lines of communication (rivers).

Special Boat Teams employ a variety of surface combatant craft to conduct and support naval and joint Special Operations, riverine warfare, and coastal patrol and interdiction.

Special Boat Teams are capable of infiltrating and exfiltrating forces, providing small-caliber gunfire support, conducting coastal patrol, surveillance, harassment, and interdiction of maritime lines of communication, foreign internal defense operations, deception operations, search and rescue operations, and armed escort.

A dry-deck-shelter deck captain signals to the operator of a Mark 8 SEAL delivery vehicle to move into position to be winched down for recovery onboard the nuclear-powered submarine USS *Kamehameha* (SSN-642) during dual-shelter Special Operations training off the coast of Hawaii. *Defense Visual Information Center*

The dry-deck-shelter deck captain passes wet notes to the SDV navigator prior to the SDV's launch from the USS *Kamehameha. Defense Visual Information Center*

The SDV is now secured onto the dry-deck-shelter cradle onboard the USS *Kamehameha* as the deck captain deflates the DDS-2 buoy. *Defense Visual Information Center*

A Mark 8 SDV pilot checks the DDS-2 buoy and connects to the buoy line for recovery on the USS *Kamehameha*'s dry-deck-shelter platform. *Defense Visual Information Center*

Indoctrination

SEAL training takes place at the Naval Special Warfare Center in Coronado, California. Basic underwater demolition/SEAL (BUD/S) indoctrination is five weeks and is the bonding factor among all who wear the SEAL trident. Enlisted and officers alike go through this arduous training. Thus, when an officer is assigned to command a SEAL platoon, he is commanding because he has earned it rather than its being just another rotation in his career path. This is a mandatory course designed to give the student an understanding of the techniques and performance required of him.

The first obstacle a student faces is the BUD/S physical screen test. He must pass the test to class up and begin training. At the end of the indoctrination course, he will be given a more advanced version of the BUD/S physical screen test he must pass to enter the first phase of BUD/S.

First Phase: Basic Conditioning

First phase is eight weeks. Continued physical conditioning in the areas of running, swimming, and calisthenics grows increasingly difficult as the weeks progress. Students participate in weekly 4-mile runs in boots, as well as timed obstacle courses. They swim ocean distances up to 2 miles in fins and learn small-boat seamanship.

One task a student is expected to complete in this training requires him, with hands and ankles tied, to bob for approximately 20 minutes. He then performs a series of backflips. Next, he sinks to the bottom of the pool and

"The Only Easy Day Was Yesterday" is the phrase constantly heard in BUD/S. One look at the BUD/S obstacle course and you know why. Over the wall, under the barbed wire, up a 60-foot cargo net, rope climbs, tower climbs . . . and the list goes on. Up, down, over, under, around—until your body looks like a pretzel. Do it wrong and you go through again. Too slow and you could end up a "sugar cookie." That's when the instructor orders you out into the ocean, then makes you roll around in the sand, covering every inch of your body. "Hoo-yah o-course!"

recovers his face mask, using only his teeth. The water, like Special Operations, is unforgiving; for this reason, SEALs train as they fight and fight as they train.

The first two weeks of first phase prepare students for the third, known as "hell week." Students participate in five and one-half days of continuous training, with a maximum of four hours' sleep for the entire week. This week is designed as the ultimate test of their physical and mental motivation in first phase. During hell week, they learn the value of the mainstay of the SEAL teams: *teamwork!* The remaining five weeks are devoted to learning methods of conducting hydrographic surveys, preparing hydrographic charts, and performing basic maritime operations.

A BUD/S student kicks up some sand as he performs a low crawl under barbed wire at the obstacle course. Each iteration through the O-course is graded as the students push themselves to their limits and beyond.

Up and over: two BUD/S students climb a 60-foot cargo net. Physical training primes the future SEALs for the harsh conditions of combat in the real world.

SEALs are at home in the water. This relationship with the water begins with "drown-proofing" exercises in phase one of BUD/S training, when the student's hands are bound behind his back.

In the next step, students have their hands *and* ankles tied, and it's into the pool again. They must bob to the surface, catch a breath, then sink to the bottom of the pool. This is repeated until the future SEAL is as comfortable in the water as he is walking across the quarterdeck.

Like all Special Operations forces, SEALs are volunteers. The selection process is designed so that only the best of the best gain entry into this elite fraternity. Pictured here is "The Bell": if a BUD/S student wants to quit, three rings and he's out. Those with the motivation to gut it out are the ones who will be assets to the teams. BUD/S instructors explain, "A man who will quit in BUD/S will quit in combat, and that gets people killed." SEALs operate in small, close-knit squads, and each man must give 110 percent all the time.

Second Phase: Diving

Completing first phase proves to the instructor staff that a candidate is motivated to participate in more in-depth training. The diving phase is eight weeks. Physical training continues during this period, and the times are lowered for the 4-mile run, 2-mile swim, and obstacle course.

Second phase concentrates on combat SCUBA (self-contained underwater breathing apparatus). Students are taught two types of SCUBA: open-circuit (compressed air), which produces telltale bubbles, and closed-circuit (100 percent oxygen), which produces no bubbles. They participate in a progressive dive schedule emphasizing the basic combat swimmer skills necessary to qualify as a combat diver. These skills enable them to operate tactically and to complete their combat objective.

SEALs get extensive training in hand-to-hand combat. Here, BUD/S students go through martial arts exercises before entering the pool.

Upon successful completion of training, SEALs are awarded the coveted SEAL trident, seen here in a subdued olive drab patch worn on battle dress uniforms.

Third Phase: Land Warfare

The demolitions, reconnaissance, weapons, and tactics phase is nine weeks. Physical training grows more strenuous as the run distances increase and minimum passing times are lowered for the runs, swims, and obstacle course. Third phase concentrates on land navigation, small-unit tactics, rappelling, military land and underwater explosives, and weapons training. The final four weeks are spent on San Clemente Island, where students apply in a practical environment the techniques acquired throughout training.

Post-BUD/S Schools

BUD/S graduates receive three weeks of basic parachute training at Army Airborne School, Fort Benning, Georgia, prior to returning to the Naval Special Warfare Center for 15 weeks of SEAL qualification training.

After successfully completing SEAL qualification training, qualified personnel are awarded a Naval Special Warfare designation trident insignia and are assigned to a SEAL team. New combat swimmers serve the remainder of their first enlistment (two and a half to three years) in either a SEAL delivery vehicle (SDV) or a SEAL team.

Navy corpsmen who complete BUD/S and basic airborne training attend two weeks of Special Operations technician training. They also participate in an intense course of instruction in diving medicine and medical skills called 18D (the Special Operations medical sergeant course). This is a 30-week course where students receive training in treating burns, gunshot wounds, and trauma.

A broad range of advanced training opportunities is available. Advanced courses include sniper school, dive supervisor, language training, SEAL tactical communication, and many others. Shore duty opportunities are available in research and development, instructor duty, and overseas assignments.

SEALs also attend the U.S. Army Military Free Fall School, where they learn techniques to infiltrate via high altitude low opening (HALO) and high altitude high opening (HAHO) methods (see chapter 3).

A boat crew lifts a 250-pound IBS (inflatable boat–small) over their heads. The IBS is their constant companion during phase one of training. They learn how to propel it through the ocean, portage it over rocks, pass through surf. They also run with it over their heads, up and down the beach at Coronado. Make a mistake and the instructors just might fill the IBS with sand before your next run.

A student digs down deep to muster the strength to support his IBS. It's not just a matter of supporting the boat—he's supporting his boat crew, and that's what BUD/S is all about: *teamwork*.

A boat crew struggles to lift their IBS off the beach and back into the air. If you look into the boat, you'll see the instructors have added some motivation by shoveling sand into the small craft.

Desert Patrol Vehicle (DPV)

SEALs are known for having the "coolest" equipment and the "sexiest" weapons. When it comes to land vehicles, they bring a whole new meaning to the term "high-speed." The fast attack vehicle (FAV), a modified dune buggy fitted for three men, is officially called the desert patrol vehicle (DPV), having earned the title from action in Operation Desert Storm.

Manufactured by Chenowth Racing in California, it was introduced to military service in 1980 with the army's 9th Light Infantry Division. The conventional forces and commanders did not know or care how to exploit the

capabilities of this "Baja racer," and the program was abandoned in the mid- to late 1980s. Around this time, U.S. Special Operations Forces took delivery of a number of FAVs, and the SEALs begin to tinker with them.

The engine has four cylinders and is air-cooled. The latest version is 200 horsepower. It has an internal/external oil cooler, which is a big improvement over the DPVs used in Desert Storm. With the new oil cooler, they can run wide open in over 120-degree weather with no problems. The air cleaner is a two-stage system. No matter what conditions it is running in, the first stage stops all the dirt. The crews have never gotten any dirt out of the second stage.

The DPV has a four-speed transmission, Volkswagen style. However, the transmission has been highly modified, with only reverse being stock. This is because nobody manufactures a reverse racing gear.

The frame is polyfiber, and the cowling can be removed, depending on the mission profile. Baskets alongside the frame have multiple uses. They can store food, water, ammunition, and crew members' gear. They can accommodate collapsible fuel bladders to extend the DPV's range. They can also accommodate downed pilots. Each DPV can carry out two pilots in the case of combat search-and-rescue operations.

The DPV has skid plates all along the bottom, so rock and other ground debris doesn't have an effect on the crew or vehicle. Clearance is approximately 16 inches with 24 inches of wheel travel. Each rear wheel has four shocks. Three are working all the time; the fourth is a secondary. After the rear wheel travels a certain distance, it engages an additional set of torsion bars and the fourth shock.

A SEAL subdues a captured role-playing intruder in a cabin of the USNS *Leroy Grumman* during a visit/vessel board, search and seizure training exercise. Can you say "pretzel"? *Defense Visual Information Center*

The crew can tune the vehicle's suspension, depending on the mission, load, and terrain. The DPV can be set up to carry 2,000 pounds of gear. The seats feature a five-point harness, so the more tightly occupants strap themselves in, the less they get knocked around.

The tires of the vehicle are Mickey Thompson with bead lock. This allows the DPV to run on flat tires without the tires coming off the rims. The sidewall also features a tread pattern, so flat or not, they have traction. Along with the disc brakes, the vehicle features cutting brakes. By operating levers, the driver can brake the vehicle and place it in a sharp turn. This is extremely useful in an ambush, when the driver needs to maneuver the vehicle to get armament lined up on an enemy.

The DPV is bristling with hard points to mount and support various weapon systems. It has two racks for AT-4 anti-tank missiles and the side baskets can carry additional AT-4s. The baskets also have room for Stingers (shoulder-launched surface-to-air missiles).

The top mount accepts an M-2 .50-caliber machine gun or a Mark 19 40mm grenade launcher. The front mount for the operator riding shotgun

Each DPV can carry out two pilots in combat search-and-rescue operations.

normally accepts a 7.62mm light machine gun but will also accept a Mark 19, giving the crew substantial fire-power. With Mark 19s mounted both top and front, the crew can put out over 180 rounds downrange in less than 30 seconds. This is often referred to as "steel rain."

The DPV also has a rear mount for an M60A3 or other light machine gun. The primary use for this weapon is to break contact with enemy forces.

Special Boat Team craft include the Mark V, the rigid inflatable boat (RIB), and PC-class ships.

A member of SEAL Team Five shows a clear view of the 40mm grenade vest, which will hold 24 of the projectiles. The assortment of 40mm grenades includes high-explosive dual-purpose, tactical cs, star parachute, star cluster, ground marker, and practice rounds. The M203 grenade launcher, attached to his rifle is a single-shot, breech-loading, pump-action (sliding barrel), compact weapon, capable of engaging targets to 400 meters.

Many SOF units are upgrading to the M240 series of machine gun to replace the aging M60 series. However, you will still find a number of modified M60 machine guns in the SEAL armory. The M60A3 has a shorter barrel and forward vertical pistol grip, to aid in aiming the weapon. Once regarded as a crew-served weapon, the M60A3 can be manned by a single SEAL and is capable of being fired from the shoulder with remarkable accuracy. Nothing says suppressive fire like a continuous stream of 7.62mm rounds.

Mark V

The Mark V is used to insert and extract SOF units in general and SEALs in particular. With a speed in excess of 45 knots and an array of assorted weapons, the boat crews can lay down suppressive fire to support extraction of operators from a "hot" pickup zone. The Mark V weighs 57 tons and can be delivered in-theater by C-5 aircraft.

The Mark V Special Operations craft is the newest in the naval special warfare inventory. Its primary mission is as a medium-range insertion and extraction platform for Special Operations Forces in a low- to medium-threat environment. The secondary mission is limited coastal patrol and interdiction. It normally operates in a two-craft detachment with a mobile support team, which provides technical assistance and maintenance.

The typical mission duration is 12 hours. The Mark V is fully interoperable with Patrol Coastal–class ships and rigid inflatable boats. Therefore, all could be employed from a forward-operating base in a synergistic effect. A Mark V detachment, consisting of two craft and support equipment, can be deployed on two USAF C-5 aircraft into a theater within 48 hours of notification.

The Mark V Special Operations craft is the newest in the Naval Special Warfare inventory.

Seated at the controls of the Mark V is a special warfare combatant-craft crewman. These troops, which are neither SEALs nor SDV team members, support SEALs and other Special Operations Forces during maritime and riverine missions and conduct unconventional small-boat operations.

The Mark V's primary mission is to act as a medium-range insertion and extraction platform for Special Operations Forces in a low- to medium-threat environment.

Rigid Inflatable Boat (RIB)

This 11-meter boat delivers SEALs from ship to shore and is the primary naval special warfare craft for insertion and extraction of SEALs. This high-speed craft is faster, stealthier, and has a longer range than its predecessors. The larger model can accommodate an entire squad of SEALS.

The rigid inflatable boat is a high-speed, high-buoyancy, extreme-weather craft primarily used to insert and extract SEAL tactical elements from enemy-occupied beaches. The boat is constructed of glass-reinforced plastic with an inflatable-tube gunwale made of a new Hypalon neoprene/nylon-reinforced fabric. Two sizes of RIBs are currently in inventory: a 24-foot and a 30-foot.

The rigid inflatable boat has demonstrated the ability to operate in light-loaded condition in sea state 6 and winds of 45 knots. For other than heavy-weather coxswain training, operations are limited to sea state 5 and winds of 34 knots or less.

Mark V Specifications

Length: 81 feet, 2 inches

Beam: 17 feet, 5 3/4 inches

Draft: 5 feet

Displacement: 57 tons (full load)

Fuel capacity: 2,600 gallons

Propulsion: 2 MTU 12V396 diesels (2,285 horsepower each); 2 waterjets

Hull: Aluminum, with five watertight compartments

Radar: Full suite communications (HF, UHF, HF, SATCOM), GPS, IFF

Complement: 1 officer, 5 enlisted

Detachment: 16 SOF combat-loaded operators with 4 combat rubber raiding craft

Performance: (Maximum speed) 45 to 48 knots for 250 nautical miles in sea state 2; (cruising speed) 25 to 40 knots in sea state 3

Maximum range: 500 nautical miles (2 engines at 45 knots)

Armament: Any combination of .50-caliber machine guns, M60 machine guns, Mark 19 grenade launchers, and other small arms

Possible future modifications: Mounting stations for GAU-17 minigun, Mark 95 twin .50-caliber machine gun, and/or Mark 38 chain gun

Patrol Coastal (PC)–Class Ships

Naval special warfare has taken control of 12 of 13 Patrol Coastal (PC)–class ships. The PC class operates in low-intensity environments and has a primary mission of coastal patrol and interdiction, with a secondary mission of naval special warfare support.

Coastal patrol and interdiction includes forward presence, monitoring and detection operations, escort operations, noncombatant evacuation, and foreign internal defense. Naval special warfare operational missions include long-range SEAL insertions and extractions, tactical swimmer operations, intelligence collection, operational deception, and coastal or riverine support.

PCs normally operate as a two-boat detachment. This allows enhanced support and facilitates the assignment of one mobile support team for every two ships.

Vietnam

Formed in 1962, the SEALs were the navy's answer to the Army Special Forces troops, or "Green Berets." However, the men and missions were at the extreme ends of the special warfare spectrum. While the Green Berets' primary mission was to win the hearts and minds of the Vietnamese people, the SEALs' primary mission was to hunt, ambush, and kill the elusive Viet Cong.

The most feared animal in the jungles of Vietnam was that Navy SEAL. The Viet Cong and North Vietnamese Army (NVA) were in a constant state of fear, never knowing when the SEALs would appear out of nowhere and attack. The NVA were perplexed as to who these waterborne soldiers were. They were not army troops, because they did not attack en masse. They could not be marines, because they did not dig in and build base camps. Their origins unknown, the enemy referred to the Navy SEALs as the "men with green faces," a reference to the green and black camouflage makeup the commandos applied to their faces before missions. These waterborne commandos would conduct ambush and prisoner snatch operations well back from main rivers and trails and deep behind enemy territory, beating him at his own game.

Grenada

On 25 October 1983, Operation Urgent Fury began as the United States invaded the Caribbean island of Grenada. The island had been under expanding Cuban influence for some time. Following a failed military coup to overthrow

Rigid Inflatable Boat Specifications

	Small RIB	Large RIB
Length	24 feet	30 feet
Beam	9 feet	11 feet
Draft	2 feet	3 feet
Weight	9,300 pounds	14,700 pounds
Propulsion	Single Volvo Penta	Two Iveco Diesels with waterjets
Complement	3 crew/4 passengers	3 crew/8 passengers
Radar	HF, UHF, VHF	HF, UHF, VHF, SATCOM
Performance	25-plus knots	35-plus knots
Range	170 nautical miles	200 nautical miles
Seaworthiness	Sea state 5	Sea state 5
Armament	Forward and after mounts capable of M60	Forward and after mounts capable of M-60, M-2, or Mark 19

the communist leader Maurice Bishop, President Ronald Reagan was concerned for the safety of the hundreds of Americans on the island. He therefore determined that an invasion was the preferred option to restore stability on the island

The first of two SEAL missions was the assault on the governor-general's mansion in the St. George area. The governor-general was never in dire danger, and the SEALs sustained only one wounded in this action, which led to numerous People's Revolutionary Army casualties and U.S. military wounded in action. The second mission was reconnaissance of the beach landing site and area adjacent to Pearls Airport at the northern end of the island.

The Grenada operation was not without its cost to the Special Operations community. Four SEALs were lost at sea during a rubber-duck insertion (i.e., a combat rubber raiding craft pushed from a helicopter, with the SOF team following). This tragedy would hit hard across the Special Operations Forces community. Operation Urgent Fury was also fraught with problems caused by poor planning and lack of standardization among the special operation units.

PC-Class Ships Specifications

Length: 170 feet

Beam: 25 feet

Draft: 7.8 feet

Displacement: 328.5 tons (full load)

Fuel capacity: 18,000 gallons

Propulsion: 4 Paxman diesels (3,350 horsepower each)

Generators: 2 Caterpillar (155 kilowatts each)

Hull: Steel, with aluminum superstructure

Sensors and navigation systems: Commercial

Complement: 4 officers, 24 enlisted

Detachment: Berthing for nine-man SOF/law-enforcement detachment

Performance: (Maximum speed) 30-plus knots; (cruising speed) 12 knots

Seaworthiness: Survive through sea state 5

Maximum range: In excess of 3,000 nautical miles (2 engines at 16 knots)

Armament: Mark 38 25mm rapid fire gun, Mark 96 25mm rapid fire gun, Stinger station, four pintles supporting any combination of .50-caliber machine guns, M60 machine guns, and Mark 19 grenade launchers

Small arms: Mark 52 Mod 0 chaff decoy launching system

Preplanned product improvement: Naval special warfare RIB retrieval system

MISSIONS

Panama

In December 1989, the United States began Operation Just Cause, the invasion of Panama. One of the primary missions was to hunt down and capture General Manuel Noriega, the country's dictator, who was also a drug dealer. Because of concerns that Noriega might attempt to flee the country, the SEALs were tasked with two missions to prevent his escape, to be carried out prior to the invasion, or H-Hour.

The first mission was to disable the general's boats, which were considered a means of escape. Under cover of darkness, the SEALs infiltrated Balboa Harbor, where the power yachts *Macho de Monte I* and *Macho de Monte II* were moored. Using Draeger closed-circuit rebreathers, the waterborne commandos entered the water and approached the vessels.

One team placed limpet mines on the stern of one boat, while the second team placed C-4 plastic explosive around the twin propeller shafts of the other boat. The SEALs set the timers and exfiltrated the harbor, swimming to their teammates waiting for them in combat rubber raiding craft. Twenty minutes later, a thunderous explosion ripped through the night, and the two boats had been removed from any escape plan. Mission accomplished!

Unfortunately, the other SEAL mission did not share the same success. This involved taking Patilla Airfield and destroying Noriega's Learjet, eliminating yet another escape route. Although the SEALs are highly skilled in war fighting, Army Rangers, rather than Navy SEALs, are the ones who take down airports. However, this was the mission they drew, and they would do what was necessary to accomplish the task.

Although SEALs normally work in small teams, usually an 8-man squad or 16-man platoon, the raid on Patilla called for three platoons, or 48 SEALs. Flawed from the beginning, the mission was further compromised

"Mission complete. Request exfil." A SEAL platoon leader instructs his radioman to contact the extraction helicopter, advising it that they are ready for withdrawal. The SEALs have "thrown smoke" to identify their position for the inbound helicopter.

when the invasion began 15 minutes before schedule. The element of surprise, which the SEALs depend on, had been lost.

Nevertheless, they "drove on." Now they were not infiltrating a quiet airfield, but an airport where soldiers of the Panamanian Defense Force (PDF) were on alert and waiting for them.

As they neared the hanger housing the Learjet, a PDF soldier came out of the hanger and approached the SEALs, suggesting that they lower their weapons. The SEALs strongly suggested that the PDF drop their weapons. Within moments, the PDF opened fire. The SEALs, who had no cover on the open tarmac, returned fire. In the course of the firefight, one of the SEALs took out Noriega's Learjet with an AT-4 antitank weapon.

The mission had been accomplished, but at a high cost: six of the SEALs had been killed and eight others seriously wounded. After this mission, new operational criteria were established for employing Special Operations Forces units: Is this an appropriate SOF mission? Does it support the theater commander's campaign plan? Is it operationally feasible? Are the required resources available? Does the expected outcome justify the risk?

Had these questions been asked prior to the Patilla raid, the SEALs would never have been committed to such actions. As a result, the SEAL platoon is the largest operational element that will normally be employed to conduct a tactical mission. Multiplatoon operations are avoided after the Patilla disaster.

Kuwait

During Operation Desert Storm in February 1991, Navy SEALs conducted a mission critical to the success of General Norman H. Schwarzkopf's "Hail Mary" plan. One of the Iraqis' concerns was that the U.S. would mount an amphibious invasion on the shores of Kuwait. These concerns were solidified when the marines openly practiced for such a contingency.

The icing on the cake was a deception mission assigned to Navy SEALs. After numerous reconnaissance operations over the coastline, the location was selected and the mission approved. In command of the SEAL platoon was Lieutenant Tom Dietz. He and his men infiltrated the Kuwaiti shore, where they planted satchel charges containing prepared amounts of C-4 explosives.

SEALs operate in small teams and are not equipped for sustained, direct engagements against enemy forces. The nature of SEAL missions requires the platoons to carry minimum amounts of equipment, munitions, and light armament, consisting primarily of individual weapons. Although it may be considered light by SOF standards, SEALs carry more ammunition and firepower than an average conventional infantry company. Surprise and aggressiveness on target are essential to the success of Special Operations.

In addition to the demolitions, they strung out buoys, marking amphibious landing zones to the beach. To complete the ruse, navy ships and aircraft were added to the operation. At 0100 on 24 February 1991, the satchel charges detonated, confirming the Iraqis' worst fears that the marines were landing.

Saddam Hussein diverted two Iraqi divisions to the seaside, to await an invasion that never materialized. This diversion of enemy troops allowed the U.S. and coalition forces to swing west and into Iraq, dealing a devastating blow to the Iraqis—all made possible by a handful of SEALs.

Afghanistan

Navy SEALs conducted special reconnaissance on suspected al-Qaeda and Taliban forces throughout the Afghanistan region during Operation Enduring Freedom. SEAL teams performed a wide variety of missions, including sensitive site exploitation and search-and-destroy missions. The platoons found themselves in caves, houses, compounds, and underground complexes. Such responsibilities netted the SEALs tons of ammunition, weapons, and intelligence material on the terrorist forces.

A "sensitive site" is a geographically limited area with special diplomatic, informational, military, or economic sensitivity to the United States. Examples of such sites would be suspected plants, research facilities, or warehouses containing weapons of mass destruction, whether nuclear, biological, or chemical. Other such sites are those where high-ranking enemy forces or regime leaders might be located.

Iraq

During Operation Iraqi Freedom, Navy SEALs using high-speed Mark V special warfare craft of the Special Boat Team assaulted two Iraqi offshore oil platforms, Mina al Bakar and Khawr al Amaya, in the Persian Gulf. As the waterborne commandos assaulted the platforms, snipers provided cover fire from orbiting helicopters. The seizure of these oil platforms assured that Saddam Hussein's forces could not repeat the ecological assault of the first Gulf War, when they dumped raw crude oil into the Persian Gulf. The SEALs were also instrumental in clearing mines from the waterways that impeded naval and humanitarian vessels, as well as other missions.

Lieutenant j.g. John Morris, U.S. Navy SEAL, readies his gear for a visit, board, search, and seizure. His primary weapon is an HK MP5, appropriate for close-quarter battle. MP5 submachine guns can still be found in the SEALs' inventory and are well suited for shipboard operations, where a higher-velocity round, such as the 5.56mm ammunition of the M4A1 carbine, might ricochet off the ship's bulkheads. *Defense Visual Information Center*

CHAPTER 3

U.S. Army
Special Forces

Motto: De Oppresso Liber
(To Liberate the Oppressed)

The men of the U.S. Army Special Forces, otherwise known as "Green Berets," are highly adaptable in their fighting techniques. Their primary mission is training guerrilla forces behind enemy lines. Introduced in the unconventional warfare role, they adjusted remarkably to counterinsurgency as well as dealing with conventional warfare and civilian irregulars. The five core missions of the U.S. Army Special Forces are direct action, special reconnaissance, unconventional warfare, foreign internal defense, and counterterrorism. Whether defending isolated camps in Afghanistan with members of the Northern Alliance Forces or operating on a small SOF team in the deserts of Iraq, Special Forces soldiers are highly motivated and possess the determination to accomplish their missions at all costs.

All Special Forces soldiers are airborne qualified. This method of insertion is learned at Basic Airborne School at Fort Benning, where the instructors convert their ground-bound students into paratroopers.

Previous page: Headquarters for the U.S. Army Special Operations Command is at Fort Bragg, North Carolina.

Today, the U.S. Army Special Forces Command (Airborne), USASFC(A), includes seven major subordinate units (or groups), each commanded by a colonel. The mission statement of the Special Forces Command is "To organize, equip, train, validate, and prepare forces for deployment to conduct worldwide Special Operations, across the range of military operations, in support of regional combatant commanders, American ambassadors, and other agencies as directed." The multifold missions of diplomat, teacher, and warrior have earned the soldiers of the U.S. Army Special Forces the title "the quiet professionals."

A member of the 3rd SFG(A) armed with an M4A1 assault rifle provides cover while his teammates emerge from the brush and continue their infiltration. Depending on the mission and area of operations, many Special Forces soldiers will camouflage their weapons to promote their clandestine activity.

The five core missions of the U.S. Army Special Forces are direct action, special reconnaissance, unconventional warfare, foreign internal defense, and counterterrorism. Here, members of the 3rd SFG(A) demonstrate a "hasty ambush" technique.

HISTORY

Today's Special Forces are founded on a rich heritage and warrior lineage. Modern SF soldiers draw their combat skills from the proud tradition of their special warfare predecessors: Francis Marion, the "Swamp Fox;" the Office of Strategic Services (OSS) Jedburgh teams; 1st Special Service Forces, and others.

Special Operations units, as envisioned by two colonels—Colonel Aaron Bank in particular, along with Colonel Russell Volckmann—would be a force multiplier. These small teams, with striking similarities to today's Special Forces A-detachments, would operate behind the enemy's lines and raise havoc and confusion within his ranks. It would be possible for a handful of men to effectively hamper, disrupt, and paralyze a much larger conventional force, such as the Soviets.

The new organization would be referred to as "Special Forces," the name derived from the operational groups the OSS fielded in 1944. In the spring of 1952, Colonel Bank headed to Fort Bragg, North Carolina, to choose the location for a psychological warfare/Special Forces center. He then began bringing together selected officers and NCOs who would serve as the nucleus of the new organization.

From its inception, only the best troops were sought, and Bank got them. Among the ranks assembled in the new organization were former OSS officers, airborne troops, Ranger troops, and combat veterans from World War II and Korea. Although the Rangers were already part of a similar air force group, Rangers units had a habit of being decommissioned between wars, and these soldiers wanted to be in an active special unit.

After months of concentrated preparation the new unit was ready, and on 19 June 1952, the 10th Special Forces Group (Airborne) was activated under the command of Colonel Aaron Bank. On the day of its activation, the 10th SFG(A) had a total complement of ten soldiers, Colonel Bank, one warrant officer, and eight enlisted men. Within months, hundreds of additional volunteers reported to Smoke Bomb Hill after completing the initial phase of their Special Forces training.

A member of the 10th Special Forces Group (Airborne) provides security while his team members prepare their base camp. He is armed with an M4A1 carbine. Attached to the weapon is the vertical hand grip and the advanced combat optical gunsight (ACOG) four-power scope. These attachments are from the Special Operations peculiar modifications (SOPMOD) kit.

As soon as the group was large enough, Bank started training his soldiers in the most advanced unconventional warfare techniques. The group's initial mission was to infiltrate operational detachments by land, sea, or air to designated areas behind the enemy's line—some to Korea, and most to Europe, to counter the Soviet threat.

The purpose was to establish and train indigenous forces to conduct Special Forces operations, with an emphasis on guerrilla warfare. They also had secondary missions, including deep-penetration raids, intelligence-gathering assignments, and counterinsurgency operations. It was asking a lot and demanded a commitment to professionalism and excellence unparalleled in the history of America's military, but the men of the 10th Special Forces Group (Airborne) were up to the challenge.

Members of the U.S. Army Special Forces still espouse the ideal held up by President John F. Kennedy. He gave the men of the Special Forces more than the green beret—he gave them a mission: uphold democracy at all costs. Over the past five decades, this ideal has been carried into various conflicts, and the men of the Special Forces have paid the price. At the height of the Vietnam War, there were over a dozen Special Forces Groups, including active, Army Reserve, and National Guard units.

Special Forces soldiers may be deployed into third world countries to train their military forces. For this reason, SF soldiers are also trained in vintage weapons, such as this World War II-era M3 .45-caliber submachine gun.

Two members of the 10th Special Forces Group (Airborne) check their position with the aid of the Global Positioning System. Special Forces teams are often tasked with being the eyes and ears of a theater commander. Whether winding their way through a snake-infested jungle or high upon a snow-covered mountaintop, the men of the Special Forces are experts at executing their missions.

Structure

There are five active Special Forces Groups, oriented to specific areas around the world. By concentrating on specific regions, SF soldiers gain experience in the regional cultures and languages of their assigned countries. This also gives them the opportunity to form a bond with the foreign military forces and a working relationship with the indigenous population.

The 1st Special Forces Group (Airborne) is headquartered at of Fort Lewis, Washington. The 1st SFG(A) also provides soldiers for Detachment K, or Det-K, based in Korea, including two active-duty and two reserve chemical-recon detachments (these chemical detachments are not SF personnel) and a 13-man SF detachment. These units support theater war-planning requirements on the Korean peninsula. Their area of responsibility (AOR) is the Pacific rim and Asia. They operate under PACCOM, or the Pacific Command.

Members of the 5th Special Forces Group (Airborne) use a Barrett M82A1 to practice long-range firing in the desert. It is fitted with a Swarovski 10-power scope.

Beret Flashes of the U.S. Army Special Operations (Left to Right): Top Row: U.S. Army Special Operations Command (Airborne), U.S. Army Special Forces Command (Airborne), U.S. Army John F. Kennedy Special Warfare Center & School (Airborne), and U.S. Army Special Warfare Training Group (Airborne). Middle Row (Active): 1st Special Forces Group (Airborne), 3rd Special Forces Group (Airborne), 5th Special Forces Group (Airborne), 7th Special Forces Group (Airborne), and 10th Special Forces Group (Airborne). Bottom Row (National Guard):19th Special Forces Group (Airborne) and 20th Special Forces Group (Airborne).

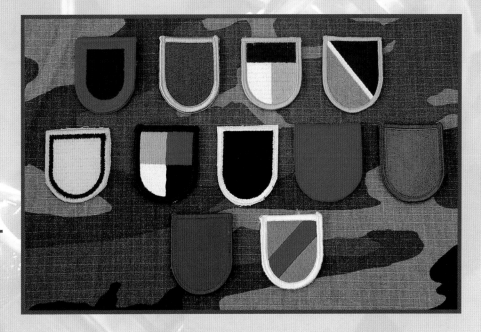

The 3rd SFG(A) is based at Fort Bragg, North Carolina, concentrating mainly on the continent of Africa, excluding the Horn of Africa. Third Group also has one battalion that is on line to support CENTCOM (Central Command), which is responsible for the Middle East.

The 5th SFG(A) is located at Fort Campbell, Kentucky, and is the lead Group under CENTCOM. Their area of responsibility is from the Horn of Africa up through the Central Asian republics of Kazakhstan, Turkmenistan, and Tajikistan.

Also headquartered at Fort Bragg is the 7th SFG(A), which operates in Central and South America and the Caribbean, the SOUTHCOM (South Command) area of responsibility.

Finally, the 10th Special Forces Group (Airborne) is based at Fort Carson, Colorado. Its EUCOM (European Command) area of responsibility comprises Europe and countries of the former Soviet Union, including Russia. The 10th Group holds the honor of being the original SF group.

There are two National Guard SF groups: the 19th SFG(A), headquartered in Salt Lake City, Utah, with units spread throughout the western United States, and the 20th SFG(A), with headquarters in Birmingham, Alabama, with units throughout the eastern United States. When you total all the personnel, you end up with approximately 1,200 per SF group, or 10,000 worldwide.

Each Special Forces company has six Operational Detachment-Alphas (ODAs, described later in this chapter). One is a HALO team, schooled in military freefall, one is a SCUBA team, trained as combat swimmers, and one is a counterterrorist team. Some of the battalions also have a mobility team. The remaining teams are referred to as *ruck* teams (for *rucksack*) and use the "low-impact" method of insertion: by foot. All teams are trained in fast-roping, or FRIES.

When the word is given, the third man in the stack will blow the door, and before the smoke has settled, the counterterrorist team will have entered and neutralized the targets.

Milliseconds after the charge is triggered, the door disintegrates into splinters, leaving an unhindered entryway for the team to ingress the building.

Mobility

Mounted teams use the ground mobility vehicle (GMV), which had its origins in Desert Storm. Special Forces use a modified HUMMV (dubbed DUMMV, pronounced "dum-vee"), for extended desert missions. The modifications include a heavier suspension, a more powerful engine, and an open bed to store water, fuel, and other mission-essential items.

The GMV has a cupola on top, similar to the one used to mount a TOW antitank missile system, used to mount various weapons systems, such as an M2 .50-caliber machine gun and a Mark 19 40mm grenade machine gun.

The crew for an SF mounted team is three men per GMV, with four GMVs per team. The GMV greatly enhances the capability of mounted teams, extending their mission endurance and flexibility.

Operational Detachment-Alpha

Operational Detachment-Alpha (ODA), also referred to as an A-Team, remains the essence of the U.S. Army Special Forces. ODAs are the soldiers on the ground who penetrate deep inside enemy territory. ODAs are designed to organize, train, advise, direct, and support indigenous military or paramilitary forces in unconventional warfare and foreign internal defense operations. An ODA is capable of training a force up to a battalion in size.

The ODA consists of 12 men: 2 officers and 10 noncommissioned officers. The ODA is commanded by a captain, who may also command or advise up to a battalion size of indigenous combat troops. He is tasked with mission planning, working with the team specialists to establish the best strategy for mission success. As the leader, he is accountable for everything that happens on that team, right or wrong.

The captain must be proficient in tasks that support the detachment's missions and possess a broad understanding of other tasks. He must also be able to operate in concert with conventional forces in large-scale operations.

Members of 3rd SFG move to the wood line after a Fast Rope insertion.

Members of ODA-581 are active in the Central Command area of operations. One of their specialties is ground mobility. For this, they employ the ground mobility vehicle (GMV), which had its origins in Desert Storm.

The executive officer (XO) is the detachment technician, a warrant officer, and serves as second in command, ensuring that the detachment commander's decisions are implemented. His tasks include administrative and logistical portions of area studies, briefbacks and operational plans (OPLANs), and operational orders (OPORDs). In the event the mission requires the ODA to run a "split team op," the XO commands one of these teams.

The noncommissioned officers consist of two operations and intelligence sergeants, two weapons sergeants, two demolition/engineer sergeants, two communications sergeants, and two medical sergeants. This configuration allows the A-Team to operate in two six-man teams, or "split A-Teams," if necessary. It can be further broken down into six two-man teams. It is standard operating procedure that each member of the A-team is crossed trained in the SF skills.

The operations sergeant is the senior NCO on the detachment; he advises the ODA commander on all training and operational matters. The operations and intelligence sergeant, a sergeant first class, directs the ODA's intelligence training, collections, analysis, and dissemination. He assists the operations sergeant in preparing area

The executive officer (XO), a warrant officer, is second in command on an A-Team. The operations and intelligence sergeant directs the ODA's intelligence training, collections, analysis, and dissemination.

studies, briefbacks, and so on. He is responsible for field interrogation of enemy prisoners. He briefs and debriefs SF and indigenous patrols and fills in for the operations sergeant when necessary.

The two weapons sergeants, a sergeant first class and a staff sergeant, are responsible for employment of weapons, using conventional and unconventional warfare tactics and techniques. They are trained in over eighty different weapons and train indigenous troops as well as other team members in the use of small arms (pistols, rifles, assault weapons), crew-served weapons (machine guns, mortars), antiaircraft (Stingers) and antitank (light antitank weapon, AT-4) weapons.

A light weapons sergeant fires a 7.62mm M240 machine gun.

A heavy-weapons sergeant prepares to fire an AT-4 antitank weapon.

The two engineer sergeants supervise, lead, plan, perform, and instruct in all aspects of combat engineering and light construction. They are knowledgeable in demolitions and improvised munitions.

Two communications sergeants install, operate, and maintain FM, AM, HF, VHF, and SHF radio communications in voice, continuous wave (CW), and burst radio nets. They train members of the ODA and indigenous personnel in the use and maintenance of the communication equipment. They can advise, train, and command indigenous forces up to a company in size.

The final members of the ODA are two medical sergeants who provide emergency, routine, and long-term medical treatment for the ODA and associated allied or indigenous forces. They train, advise, and direct detachment members and indigenous forces in emergency medicine and preventive medical care. On prolonged missions, they establish a medical facility and are also trained in veterinary care. One other unique capability of the medical sergeants is that they are fully schooled in SF skills and are combatants. Like the other team members, they are capable of training and commanding up to a company-sized force.

Two engineer sergeants supervise all aspects of combat engineering and light construction. They are knowledgeable in demolitions and improvised munitions. They plan and perform sabotage operations.

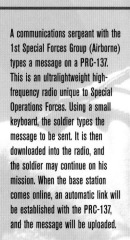

A communications sergeant with the 1st Special Forces Group (Airborne) types a message on a PRC-137. This is an ultralightweight high-frequency radio unique to Special Operations Forces. Using a small keyboard, the soldier types the message to be sent. It is then downloaded into the radio, and the soldier may continue on his mission. When the base station comes online, an automatic link will be established with the PRC-137, and the message will be uploaded.

Two medical sergeants provide emergency, routine, and long-term medical treatment for the ODA and associated allied or indigenous forces.

 # TRAINING

The JFK Special Warfare Center and School is responsible for Special Operations training. The Center and School's training group conducts the full spectrum of training in Special Operations.

The 1st Battalion conducts Special Forces assessment and selection and the SF qualification course, or Q-course.

The 2nd Battalion is responsible for advanced SF skills: military free fall (MFF); combat diving (SCUBA); survival escape, resistance, and evasion (SERE) course; Special Operations target interdiction (SOTIC) course; Special

An inside view of the medical bag of an 18D (a medic). From combat wounds to delivering a baby, the SF medical sergeant is a specialist in his field. He is responsible for the well-being of the ODA and indigenous forces. There are times when he is the only medically trained person some people in a third world country will ever see.

Land navigation is one of the most important skills a Special Forces soldier possesses. While modern technology may offer pinpoint positioning, each Special Forces soldier must be an expert with a map and a compass. Navigation skills are emphasized in all phases of Special Forces training.

Every Special Forces soldier goes through language training. Here, Special Forces soldiers use computer self-paced study programs to learn an assortment of languages. Other students will be in classes with actual instructors from Mexico, South America, Thailand, Korea, or a dozen other countries. By using native speakers as instructors, soldiers not only learn the indigenous language and intonation but also the traditions and customs of that nation

Forces advanced reconnaissance, target analysis and exploitation techniques course (SFARTAETC); and advanced Special Operations techniques (ASOT). The urbanization of the combat environment has also resulted in the creation of the Special Forces advanced urban combat (SFAUC) training, which is advanced close-quarter battle for tactical missions.

The 3rd Battalion teaches civil affairs, psychological operations, and languages and regional area studies that Special Forces warrant officers need.

Camp MacKall is where the potential Special Forces soldier begins his trip, with Special Forces assessment and selection. Candidates undergo physical and psychological evaluation as well as the basic skills of the Special Forces soldier. Soldiers who pass continue to the Q-course for further training in the capabilities of the A-Team.

Special Forces Assessment and Selection (SFAS)

The purpose of Special Forces assessment and selection is to identify soldiers who have the potential for Special Forces training. SFAS is conducted by the 1st Battalion, 1st SWTG(A) at Rowe Training Facility, Camp MacKall, near Fort Bragg. Every prospective Special Forces soldier must successfully complete the 24-day SFAS program. Training includes:

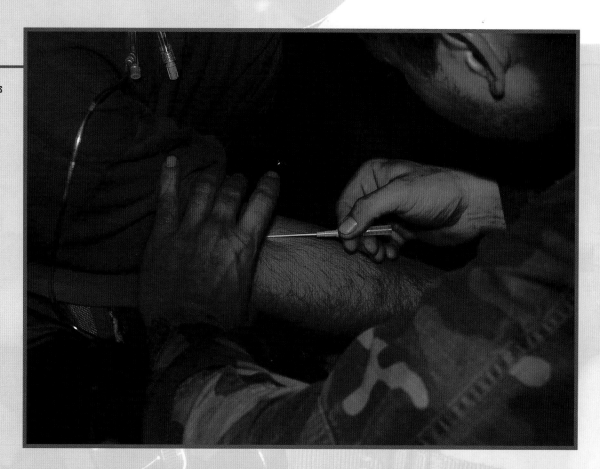

Special Forces medic sergeants are some of the best-trained medical specialists in the U.S. military. A medic student administers an IV to one of the guerrillas during a Robin Sage exercise.

Special Forces engineers teach not only how to build structures, bridges, and so on, but also how to "blow things up." Here we see a student engineer sergeant measuring a length of fuse to meet the timing requirements for the explosive charge he will set during a direct action raid.

SF detachment commanders learn the planning and leadership skills they will need to direct and employ other members of their detachments: escape and recovery; infiltration (infil) and extraction (exfil); MOS training in weapons, engineering, medicine, and communications; military decision making; terrain analysis; direct action; special reconnaissance; foreign internal defense; and unconventional warfare.

SF weapons sergeants learn the characteristics and capabilities of over 89 types of U.S. and foreign light weapons (handguns, submachine guns, rifles, machine guns, mortars, antitank weapons, and man-portable air defense weapons); range planning; tactics; indirect fire operations; weapons emplacement; and integrated combined arms fire control planning.

SF engineer sergeants learn not only how to construct buildings, bridges, and field fortifications, but also the best way to use demolitions for their destruction.

SF medical sergeants go through the Special Operations combat medic course, which includes a curriculum of concentrated medical training specifically designed for Special Operations medical personnel, including pararescumen, SEALs, and Rangers. In the second part of their training, they are assigned to hands-on patient care in emergency and hospital settings during a four-week assignment in numerous hospitals in large metropolitan areas. SF medics learn to handle many medical tasks, from combat trauma to delivering a baby, including dentistry and veterinary skills.

SF communications sergeants learn the basic skills and knowledge required to perform communications duties on a Special Forces ODA.

A communications student fashions a field-expedient antenna for the team's radio. Using some branches, a few MRE spoons, some 550 cord, and communication wire, he will be able to construct an antenna that will allow the team to extend their range of communication.

Weapons specialists receive training in over 89 weapon systems—light and heavy, U.S. and foreign. They will know how to field-strip and repair these weapons, as well as how the guerrillas may best employ them.

Robin Sage

After completing SF training, soldiers are placed into A-Teams and are ready to take their final exam. This last exercise is known as the Robin Sage and takes place in the fictional country of Pineland. The student ODA must link up with the guerrillas, also know as "Gs," and train them in unconventional warfare techniques.

Depending on their mission profile, ODAs are inserted by various methods and begin their infil to their rendezvous with the Pineland guerrillas. After a day or two, depending on the scenario and how good the team is, they make contact with the guerrilla force. If they thought humping an 80–100 pound rucksack for the last day or so was rough, it was nothing compared to the task ahead: meeting the guerrilla chief, played by an experienced SF soldier—usually a senior NCO or perhaps a retired SF soldier brought in to test the students.

In BUD/S "hell week," sleep deprivation is high on the list, and the exercise is 90 percent physical. In contrast, Robin Sage lasts two weeks, participants get a few more hours of sleep, and, while it is physically demanding, it is a thinking man's game.

Upon successful completion of the Robin Sage exercise, students are presented with the Special Forces shoulder tab and awarded the coveted green beret.

During their final exercise, known as Robin Sage, Special Forces students carry out an assortment of raids. Here, a student writes up his warning order—a list of what the mission will be. He will then instruct his assault team, made up of "role-playing" guerrillas from other services. All the time he is under the close observation of the evaluators, who determine the success or failure of the mission.

A member of the Robin Sage cadre plots the location of one of the student ODAs. Throughout the final exercise, numerous student A-Teams are scattered throughout the Uwaharrie National Forest. At cadre HQ, they keep close tabs on how the students are progressing.

Airborne

The separation of the SF trooper from his fellow soldiers begins in the hot Georgia sun. Airborne training for the prospective Special Forces trooper is conducted at the U.S. Army Airborne School at Fort Benning, Georgia, and is broken down into three phases: ground week, tower week, and jump week. Upon successful completion of airborne training, the soldier is awarded the Silver Wings, denoting he is airborne qualified and no longer a lowly LEG, a soldier who is not jump qualified. The term derives from "straight leg" and refers to the pants non-jumpers wore, which could not be bloused into their boots, unlike the pants of airborne troops.)

Instruction for military free fall begins at the U.S. Army Military Free Fall Parachutist School at Fort Bragg, culminating in Yuma, Arizona. The school's mission is to train personnel in HALO (high altitude low opening) military freefall parachuting, using the ram-air parachute system.

Special Operations Target Interdiction (SOTIC) Course

The Special Operations Target Interdiction course, as explained by Major Kim Rowe, Commander Company D, 2nd Battalion 1st SWTG(A), "trains SF personnel in the technical skills and operational procedures necessary to deliver precision rifle fire from concealed positions to selected targets in support of special operations forces missions."

This is also known as sniper training. SOTIC students are all volunteers for this training. They must have a rating of expert with their weapon, pass a number of psychological evaluations, and have Secret clearance.

SOTIC is a Level 1 category course for Special Operations Forces. This means that those who graduate from the course are qualified to instruct U.S. troops, train soldiers from foreign nations, and shoot at "close proximity" of U.S. troops and noncombatants. In simple terms, this means a SOTIC sniper can drop an enemy standing right next to you.

"One shot. One kill." A Special Forces sniper team, having completed their stalk, settles into firing position to "take out" their target. Sniper skills are important when conducting counterterrorist operations, where there is no margin for error. The team is wearing the traditional ghillie suit that allows them to blend in with their surroundings.

Special Forces Advance Reconnaissance, Target Analysis, and Exploitation Techniques Course (SFARTAETC)

This course provides basic training in the tactics, techniques, and procedures needed by personnel assigned to a theater. These skills include precision marksmanship, integrated close-quarter battle, and interpretability with other specifically designated forces.

With world terrorism a common occurrence, Special Forces have countered with a new training program called the Special Forces advance reconnaissance, target analysis, and exploitation techniques course (SFARTAETC).

Special Forces Creed

I am an American Special Forces soldier. A professional! I will do all that my nation requires of me.

I am a volunteer, knowing well the hazards of my profession. I serve with the memory of those who have gone before me: Roger's Rangers, Francis Marion, Mosby's Rangers, the first Special Service Forces, and Ranger Battalions of World War II, the Airborne Ranger Companies of Korea. I pledge to uphold the honor and integrity of all I am—in all I do.

I am a professional soldier. I will teach and fight wherever my nation requires. I will strive always, to excel in every art and artifice of war. I know that I will be called upon to perform tasks in isolation, far from familiar faces and voices, with the help and guidance of my God.

I will keep my mind and body clean, alert, and strong, for this is my debt to those who depend upon me. I will not fail those with whom I serve. I will not bring shame upon myself or the forces. I will maintain myself, my arms, and my equipment in an immaculate state as befits a Special Forces soldier.

I will never surrender though I be the last. If I am taken, I pray that I may have the strength to spit upon my enemy. My goal is to succeed in any mission—and live to succeed again.

I am a member of my nation's chosen soldiery. God grant that I may not be found wanting, that I will not fail this sacred trust.

A member of the 10th Special Forces Group (Airborne) provides security in the background while his teammate checks in with headquarters on the team's AN/PSC-5 (V) Shadowfire SATCOM radio.

Vietnam

In the early part of U.S. involvement in Vietnam, Special Forces soldiers carried out missions in which they were proficient: training a guerrilla force. According to intelligence from the CIA, SF teams were deployed to the central highlands of South Vietnam to begin training the Montagnards (a French term for "mountain people"). The Montagnards numbered over 500,000 in South Vietnam and came from approximately 20 tribes. The agency had recognized the Montagnards as possible allies in the war against the communists.

Special Forces began a program with mountain people that would become known as civilian irregular defense group (CIDG). The organization and training of this paramilitary became the primary mission for Special Forces in Vietnam. From 1961 to 1965, over eight CIDG camps were built in the isolated countryside of South Vietnam. Each outpost was self-contained and manned by a CIDG strike force, a complement of South Vietnamese Special Forces, and a U.S. Special Forces A-Team. The primary role of the A-detachments took a turn from their origins in 1952. Instead of training a guerrilla force to interdict conventional army troops, they were now training indigenous tribesmen to conduct actions against other guerrillas, the Viet Cong.

Over the course of the war, over 250 outposts of A-camps would be established throughout South Vietnam. Scattered along the Laotian and Cambodian boarders, these strategically located outposts of freedom would become a considerable thorn in the side of the Viet Cong and later the North Vietnamese Army.

Weighing a mere 2.2 pounds and small enough to fit in a battle dress uniform pocket, the M2 selectable lightweight attack munition (SLAM) is a low-volume, multipurpose munition. It is self-contained, can be easily placed, and is compatible with other munitions used for antimateriel, antivehicular, and antipersonnel purposes. It has four detonation modes: passive infrared, magnetic influence, time delay, and command detonation.

Panama

In Operation Just Cause in December 1989, Special Forces soldiers played a proactive part in the invasion, which lasted less than 24 hours.

Members of the 7th SFG(A), Company A, 3rd Battalion, under the command of Major Kevin Higgins, secured and held the Pacora River Bridge, a vital crossing point. Special Forces soldiers, along with conventional troops, blocked a Panamanian Defense Forces (PDF) vehicle convoy from bringing reinforcements across the bridge. As they held the convoy, using light antitank and AT-4 antitank weapons, an AC-130H Spectre gunship orbiting overhead employed precision fire, halting any further PDF movement.

Members of the U.S. Army Special Forces are capable of inserting by air . . .

In another part of the country, members of the 3rd Battalion were tasked with the surgical mission of disabling a television repeater facility at Cero Azul. As Operation Just Cause began on 19 December 1989, two MH-60 helicopters lifted off for their target. Aboard these two aircraft was an 18-man element of Special Forces soldiers, augmented with members of the 1109th Signal Battalion.

Once on site, they fast-roped to the ground and neutralized the target using explosives. While the signalmen went to work on the electronics equipment, the SF soldiers swept the building, making sure it was secure, and conducted patrols in the local area. They completed the mission without taking any enemy fire and were extracted by MH-60 Blackhawks.

by land . . .

by sea . . .

by sea (cont.) . . .

by sea (still cont.) . . .

Iraq

The primary mission of the Special Forces soldiers as Operation Desert Shield began was to use their foreign internal defense skills to form a defensive posture among the newly formed coalition forces.

The 5th Special Forces Group's mission of coalition assistance came to the fore. Their constant deployment in this theater and their working relation with the local military had made them familiar with the areas, languages, and cultures of these soldiers as well as their abilities and how they operated. The 10th Special Forces Group interacted with coalition members from Europe—British, French, Czech, and so on. Because of their expertise, SF soldiers worked with almost every level of coalition forces—109 battalions in total. They were instrumental in establishing a working relationship with the Saudi, Egyptian, and Syrian military.

A member of the Special Forces, "Green Berets," patrols snow-covered woods. The rifle has been camouflaged with white tape to break up the standard pattern and color of the weapon. To further aid his movement on skis, snowshoes, or mountaineering, he is equipped with an internal-frame pack. These highly skilled soldiers are trained to operate in all types of environments and in any geographical location . . .

The U.S. Army Special Forces converted their principles of coalition warfare into reality, combining the synergy of three allied corps into the coalition force that liberated Kuwait. General Norman H. Schwarzkopf, commander in chief (CinC), said of the Special Forces, "They were the glue that held the coalition together."

During Operation Desert Storm, Special Forces ODAs conducted deep reconnaissance in Saudi Arabia, Iraq, and Kuwait. These recon missions not only provided up-to-the-minute intelligence on the Iraqi forces, but included analyzing the condition of the soil to ascertain whether it would support the heavy weight of armored vehicles. In addition to the special reconnaissance mission, they performed direct action: sabotaging lines of communication; undertaking raids and ambushes; destroying command and control targets; assisting in combat search-and-rescue missions; and supporting the Kuwaiti resistance.

Special Forces ODAs continue to perform similar missions as Operation Desert Storm began the ground phase of the war. They shadowed the Iraqi Republican Guard, reporting to General Schwarzkopf's command center every move these militia made. This gave the CinC vital up-to-the-minute information required to mount the offensive that would decimate the Iraqi forces. General Schwarzkopf commented on the Special Forces teams that were placed deep into enemy territory in one of his briefings, saying, "they let us know what was going on out there, and they were the eyes out there."

jungle . . .

desert . . .

urban . . .

day . . .

night . . .

. . . around the world, around the clock. Special Forces stand poised to defend freedom on a moment's notice. From the frigid arctic winds to the humid, insect- and snake-infested jungles, the men of the Special Forces carry on in the tradition of their predecessors to defend liberty at all costs.

Haiti

During Operation Uphold Democracy, 550 Special Forces soldiers from the 3rd Special Forces Group at Fort Bragg, the 1st SFG at Fort Lewis, and two reserve component SFGs—the 19th from Colorado and the 20th from Alabama—saw service in Haiti. What was first set as an invasion of the small island turned into more of a peacekeeping mission as Special Forces soldiers manned checkpoints and performed weapons searches rather than special reconnaissance or direct action missions.

Kosovo

In Operation Joint Guardian in Kosovo in the spring of 1999, SF teams used their unique skills and cultural abilities in this region as members of the Kosovo Forces. During the early stages of American involvement, NATO planes began an air campaign over the skies of Kosovo. When a U.S. Air Force F-117 Nighthawk was shot down, members of the 10th SFG(A), who were on alert for possible combat search-and-rescue missions, were loaded into waiting helicopters within 10 minutes of getting the information on the downed pilot.

During Operation Allied Force in Kosovo, members of the 10th SFG(A) would work with Air Force Special Operations units to perform combat search-and-rescue missions.

Afghanistan

The terrain of Afghanistan made traveling by conventional methods, such as DUMMVs or all-terrain vehicles (ATVs) difficult. Also, such methods could be far from stealthy. For this reason, during Operation Enduring Freedom, SOF teams were introduced to and employed the local means of transportation: the horse. One Special Forces soldier reported that they contacted headquarters to locate an old manual on cavalry operations. SOCOM is used to getting unique requests from its operators in the field, but a request for saddles was indeed unusual.

In direct action missions, Special Forces soldiers coordinated air attacks, using state-of-the-art technology that contributed to neutralizing Taliban forces. They also directed the Northern Alliance success at Mazar-e Sharif.

During a press conference in Washington on 13 November 2001, Air Force General Richard Myers said, "U.S. special operations forces played a key role in the current Northern Alliance successes in Afghanistan. The Taliban appear to have abandoned Kabul, and some Northern Alliance forces are in the city."

Teaching multi-ethnic Afghan recruits soldiering skills may be a new development in the global war against terrorism, but for the U.S. Green Berets of the 1st Battalion, 3rd Special Forces Group (Airborne), it's a core mission they have mastered.

The Afghanistan National Army's first regular army battalion underwent 10 weeks of basic infantry and combat skills training at the Afghan Military Academy in Kabul. New recruits in the Afghan National Army received training, advice, and assistance from U.S. Army Special Forces members before commissioned and noncommissioned Afghan officers assumed responsibility. U.S. Green Berets were faced with the daunting challenge of developing the nucleus of a national army with recruits representing all provinces within Afghanistan. The unit was ready to form one new battalion every two weeks.

Operation Iraqi Freedom

In northern Iraq, Special Forces ODAs operate with the Patriotic Union of Kurdistan forces, having prepared them for battle against Iraqi army units. In the early days of Operation Iraqi Freedom, SOF forces captured a region occupied by the Ansar al-Islam, an Islamic extremist group, in northern Iraq.

From atop their mountain perch, Special Forces soldiers employed .50-caliber Barrett sniper rifles to engage the enemy positions. Over a thousand Kurdish fighters, along with approximately a hundred SOF operators, took part in the assault, rousting an estimated 650 of the Taliban-like forces funded by both Saddam Hussein and al-Qaeda. The Kurdish guerrillas, in coordinated efforts with Special Forces, also captured the cities of Mosul, Kirkuk, and Tikrit.

Brigadier General Vincent Brooks, deputy director of operations for CENTCOM, elaborated, "Our coalition special operations forces maintain pressure on the Iraqi military forces in northern Iraq through precision air strikes directed against the regular army Fifth Corps. Our searches in the Ansar al-Islam training camp continue, with coalition and Kurdish peshmerga working closely together."

CHAPTER 4

U.S. Army Rangers

Motto: Rangers Lead the Way!

The 75th Ranger Regiment, headquartered at Fort Benning, Georgia, is the army's premiere light-infantry rapid-assault force assigned to SOCOM. Their primary mission—in fact, their only mission—revolves around direct action. Their specialty is airfield seizure, though they are also more than capable of conducting raids, recovering both personnel (combat search and rescue) and special equipment, and other light infantry operations. They may be inserted and extracted by land, sea, or air. To remain proficient in all light infantry skills, Ranger units also focus on tasks such as movement to contact (i.e., moving to engage the enemy), ambush, reconnaissance, airborne and air assaults, and hasty defense.

While fast-roping is now the most widely used method of insertion, Rangers are still taught rappelling techniques. Such methods are useful for negotiating their way in mountainous terrain or down the side of a building.

The regiment maintains a constant state of readiness. Each Ranger battalion can deploy anywhere in the world with 18 hours' notice. On any given day, one Ranger Battalion is on ready reaction force (RRF) 1, with the requirement to be "wheels up" within 18 hours of notification. Additionally, one rifle company with battalion command and control can deploy in 9 hours.

HISTORY

The lineage of today's Rangers begins some 200 years ago, during the French and Indian War (1754–63). In 1756, Major Robert Rogers recruited soldiers into a unit that would number nine companies of men, referred to as Rangers. Rogers exploited unconventional warfare tactics and established them into Ranger doctrine.

Following Rogers' command, the Rangers would strike where the enemy least expected them and traverse terrain conventional forces would avoid. They would use stealth and secrecy in their movements on the enemy. Once in position, they would spring and, like a North American rattlesnake, hit fast and hard.

When it positively, absolutely, has to be destroyed, you send in the U.S. Army Rangers. When you have to seize an enemy airfield, you do it with Rangers. Their specialty is lightning raids and assaults on the enemy. *U.S. Army Special Operations Command*

Becoming a Ranger is often a starting point for further development in Army Special Operations. Here you'll find younger soldiers who are learning Special Ops skills and gaining the maturity and experience to conduct missions carried out by SOF units. *U.S. Army Special Operations Command*

Rangers operate in every environment on the planet. A trio of Rangers is seen in a forest environment. Their weapons are the M4 carbine *(standing, left)*, M4/M203 *(standing, right)* and M249 squad automatic weapon. *U.S. Army Special Operations Command*

Major Rogers instituted a plan of action to train his Rangers and personally watched over its execution. He set strict orders for his troops to follow, stressing operational security, readiness, and tactics, called "Standing Orders—Rogers Rangers:"

Don't forget nothing.

Have your musket clean as a whistle, hatchet scoured, 60 rounds powder and ball, and be ready to march at a minutes warning.

When you're on the march, act the way you would if you was sneaking up on a deer. See the enemy first.

Tell the truth about what you see and what you do. There is an army depending on us for correct information. You can lie all you please when you tell other folks about the Rangers, but don't never lie to a Ranger of office.

Don't ever take a chance you don't have to.

When we're on the march we march single file, far enough apart so one shot can't go through two men.

If we strike swamps, or soft ground, we spread out abreast, so it's hard to track us.

When we march, we keep moving till dark, so as to give the enemy the least possible chance at us.

When we camp, half the party stays awake while the other half sleeps.

Rangers operate around the world... *U.S. Army Special Operations Command*

If we take prisoners, we keep 'em separate till we have had time to examine them, so they can't cook up a story between 'em.

Don't ever march home the same way. Take a different route so you won't be ambushed.

No matter whether we travel in big parties or little ones, each party has to keep a scout 20 yards head, 20 yards on each flank, and 20 yards in the rear so the main body can't be surprised and wiped out.

Every night you'll be told where to meet if surrounded by a superior force.

Don't sit down to eat without posting sentries.

Don't sleep beyond dawn. Dawn's when the French and Indians attack.

Don't cross a river by a regular ford.

If somebody's trailing you, make a circle, come back onto your own track, and ambush the folks that aim to ambush you.

Don't stand up when the enemy's coming against you. Kneel down, lie down, hide behind a tree.

Let the enemy come till he's almost close enough to touch, then let him have it and jump out and finish him up with your hatchet.

World War II

During the Second World War, Major General Lucian K. Truscott submitted the idea of an American unit, similar to the British Commandos.

General Truscott liked the term "commandos," but he wanted something more American. In keeping with the unconventional warfare role, for troops that would meet the highest standard of courage, motivation, tenacity, fighting spirit, and ruggedness, it was only fitting to obtain a name from America's history. That name came from Major Rogers, and a new name was added to the U.S. military: Army Rangers.

On 19 June 1942, in Carrickfergus, Ireland, the 1st U.S. Army Ranger Battalion was activated under the command of Major William O. Darby. As with his predecessor, Major Rogers, the unit would come to be known as Darby's Rangers.

Darby's Rangers fought throughout Western Europe, but they achieve their greatest recognition on D-Day, 6 June 1944. The Rangers scaled the cliffs of Pointe du Hoc as part of the Allied invasion of Normandy.

Pointe du Hoc was 4 miles west of Omaha Beach, the main American landing area. It was a peninsula of steep, rocky cliffs protruding into the English Channel. Here the Germans had placed a battery of six 155mm cannons that dominated the invasion beaches. It was critical to the invasion to destroy these guns. To reach the guns the Rangers had to be inserted on a narrow shoreline, then climb up 80 to 100 foot cliffs.

Rangers are specialists in all methods of insertion techniques. A squad of Rangers navigates their Zodiac raft through a tree-covered tributary to infiltrate into enemy territory. While part of the squad paddles, the other Rangers keep a watchful eye on the surroundings.

On the morning of 6 June 1944, the three companies of Rangers plowed through heavy seas headed for the coast of Normandy. Using ropes launched by rockets, the Rangers began their perilous climb up Pointe du Hoc under a dreadful rain of enemy fire. Despite sustaining casualties, the Rangers did not let up, and within 10 minutes of the first Rangers landing on the shore, they had reached the top, establishing a foothold. These acts of heroism and determination served as a hallmark for future Ranger missions.

5307th Composite Unit

Organized in 1943, this unit of 3,000 men, all volunteers, was tasked with the mission of long-range penetration deep behind the Japanese lines. Under the leadership of Brigadier General Frank Merrill, the men of the 5307th Composite Unit (Provisional) brought the war to the Japanese in the jungles of Burma. Their objective was to destroy the enemy's jugular: their communications and supply lines. Furthermore, they were to harass and attack the Japanese at will. This unit would come to be known as Merrill's Marauders.

One of the Marauders' greatest operations was the seizure of the Myitkyina Airfield, the only all-weather airfield in the theater. Merrill and his men infiltrated through the hot, humid, insect- and disease-ridden Burmese jungle—and that was the good news. The enemy constantly outnumbered these early Rangers, and support was virtually nonexistent. The actions of Merrill's Marauders are legendary and inspirational, even by today's standards. The Marauders traversed over 1,000 miles through extremely dense jungles to accomplish their mission: attacking and securing the airfield.

While fast-roping gets the Rangers on the ground, the "extraction" part of FRIES gets them off. The soldiers attach themselves to a rope via snap links. Once they are secure, the helicopter will whisk them out of harm's way. Shown here is the snap link attached to the harness the Rangers wear.

The regiment consists of three Ranger battalions. Each battalion consists of three rifle companies of 152 Rangers each, a headquarters, and a headquarters company consisting of 124 Rangers, for a total of 580 Rangers authorized in each battalion.

Each rifle company within the regiment consists of a headquarters and headquarters company, three rifle platoons, and a weapons platoon. The weapons platoon of each rifle company contains a mortar section of two 60mm mortars and an antitank section of three three-man teams firing the 84mm Carl Gustav antitank rifle (referred to as the RAAWS: Ranger Anti-Armor Weapon System).

Of the three Ranger battalions that constitute the 75th Ranger Regiment, the 1st is located at Hunter Army Airfield, Georgia; the 2nd at Fort Lewis, Washington; and the 3rd at Fort Benning.

The weapon of choice for the Army Ranger is the Colt M4A1 assault rifle, shown here with the ACOG 4X sight and AN/PVS-14 night-vision device.

This Ranger has equipped his M4 with the M-203 40mm grenade launcher.

When Rangers need more firepower than their M4 carbines, they turn to the M249 squad assault weapon, which fires the same 5.56mm ammunition as the M4. It is normally equipped with 200 rounds of linked ammunition and, for Rangers, modified with a collapsible stock.

The current-issue sidearm is the M-9 Beretta 9mm semiautomatic pistol.

TRAINING

Benning Phase
4th Ranger Training Battalion—Fort Benning, Georgia

The Benning phase of Ranger training is designed to assess and develop the military skills, physical and mental endurance, stamina, and confidence a soldier must have to successfully accomplish combat missions. It is also designed to teach the Ranger student to properly sustain himself and his subordinates and to maintain his equipment under austere field conditions during the following phases of Ranger training

The Benning phase is executed in two parts. The first, conducted at Camp Rogers at Fort Benning, consists of an armed forces physical test and a combat water survival test, topped off with a 5-mile run; 3-mile runs with an obstacle course; a 16-mile foot march; night and day land-navigation tests; medical class; and rifle, bayonet, and hand-to-hand combat.

Rangers are capable of engaging the enemy from afar, as in the case of this sniper team . . . *U.S. Army Special Operations Command*

... or up close and personal, as demonstrated by a member of the 5th Ranger Training Brigade from Camp Merrill, Georgia. All Rangers receive training in hand-to-hand combat. Even though they are armed and equipped with the latest weapons, a Ranger is still a lethal weapon when armed with just a knife or his bare hands. Adhering to the Ranger creed, he will carry out his mission, even if he is the "lone survivor."

The advanced physical training assures physical and mental endurance and the stamina required for enhancing basic Ranger characteristics, commitment, confidence, and toughness. Additionally, the student completes the water confidence test, terrain association, demolitions, patrol base/ORP, and an airborne refresher jump.

The second part of the Benning Phase is conducted at nearby Camp William O. Darby. The emphasis is on the instruction and execution of squad combat patrol operations. The Ranger student receives instruction in boxing and fieldcraft, executes the Darby Queen obstacle course, and learns the fundamentals of patrolling, how to issue a warning order/operations order, and communications.

The fundamentals of combat patrol operations include immediate action drills, ambush and reconnaissance patrols, enter/clear a room, airborne operations, and air assault operations. This phase uses the crawl technique during the field training exercise, which allows the student to practice techniques to successfully conduct reconnaissance and ambush patrol missions. The Ranger student must then demonstrate his expertise through a series of cadre- and student-led tactical patrol operations.

Mountain Phase
5th Ranger Training Battalion—Dahlonega, Georgia

This phase is conducted in the mountains in and around Dahlonega, Georgia. During the mountain phase, students receive instruction in military mountaineering techniques as well as methods of employing a squad and platoon for combat patrol operations in a mountainous environment. They further develop their ability to command and control a platoon-size patrol through planning, preparing, and executing a variety of combat patrol missions.

Ranger students continue to learn how to sustain themselves and their teammates in the adverse conditions of the mountains. The rugged terrain, severe weather, hunger, mental and physical fatigue, and emotional stress they encounter provide the opportunity to gauge their own capabilities and limitations as well as those of their fellow students.

In addition to combat patrol operations, Ranger students receive five days of training on military mountaineering. During the first three days, they learn about knots, belays, anchor points, rope management, and the fundamentals of climbing and rappelling.

Rangers are constantly training and honing their skills to maintain their razor edge. A team of Rangers initiates their plan of attack on a targeted objective during a training exercise at the Joint Readiness Training Center. *Defense Visual Information Center*

Mountaineering training culminates with a two-day exercise at Yonah Mountain, applying the skills learned. Each student must make the prescribed climbs to continue in the course, including a 200-foot night rappel at Yonah Mountain. During the two field-training exercises, Ranger students also perform patrol missions requiring the use of their mountaineering skills.

Combat patrol missions are directed against a conventionally equipped threat force in a low-intensity conflict scenario. These patrol missions are conducted both day and night over a four-day squad field-training exercise and a platoon five-day exercise that includes moving cross-country over mountains, conducting vehicle ambushes, raiding communications/mortar sites, and conducting a river crossing or scaling a steep mountain.

Ranger students reach their objectives in several ways: cross-country movement, air assaults into small landing zones on the

Members of the 75th Ranger Regiment embark on a U.S. Air Force MH-53J Pave Low helicopter on the flight deck of the nuclear-powered aircraft carrier USS *George Washington* (CVN-73). The Rangers will provide support for a combat search and rescue during an exercise. *Defense Visual Information Center*

The M18 Claymore is a directional fragmentation mine containing 700 steel balls in a 1 1/2-pound layer of C-4 explosive. Primarily a defensive weapon, it does have a use as an offensive weapon. The mine comes with a battery tester, firing wires, and an M57 firing device.

The Claymore projects a fan-shaped pattern of steel balls in a 60-degree horizontal arc. The "kill zone" is 50 meters, with a casualty radius of 100 meters and the danger zone out to 250 meters. It is highly effective against unmounted infantry.

A member of the 6th Ranger Training Brigade practices calling in fire with an AFSOC Pave Low for a close air support (CAS) mission. Constant training allows the Rangers to maintain a high state of readiness. Steeped in a strong heritage, including notable World War II units such as Darby's Rangers and Merrill's Marauders, today's Rangers still "Lead the Way."

sides of mountains, or an 8–10-mile foot march over the Tennessee Valley Divide. The stamina and commitment of the Ranger student is stressed to the maximum. At any time, the Ranger instructors may pick out one student to lead other tired, hungry, physically expended students to accomplish yet another combat patrol mission.

Florida Phase
6th Ranger Training Battalion—Eglin Air Force Base, Florida

The third phase is conducted at Camp James E. Rudder (Auxiliary Field #6), Eglin Air Force Base. In this final phase, emphasis is on continued development of the student's combat skills. Ranger students must be capable of operating effectively under conditions of extreme mental and physical stress. This is accomplished through practical exercises in extended platoon-level patrol operations in a jungle/swamp environment. Training further develops students' ability to plan for and lead small units on independent and coordinated airborne, air assault, small-boat, ship-to-shore, and dismounted combat patrol operations in a low-intensity combat environment against a hostile force.

The Florida phase continues the progressive, realistic opposition-forces (OPFOR) scenario. As the scenario unfolds, students receive training that assists them in accomplishing the tactical missions in the phase and are updated on the scenario that eventually commits the unit to combat during techniques training. The 10-day field-training exercise is fast-paced, highly stressful, and challenging. Students are evaluated on their ability to apply small-unit tactics/techniques, such as for raids and ambushes, to accomplish their missions. Upon completion of the Florida phase, students conduct an airborne insertion into Fort Benning.

During the Ranger course, students prove they can overcome apparently overwhelming mental and physical hardships. They establish, under simulated combat conditions, that they have obtained the professional skills and techniques necessary to plan, organize, coordinate, and conduct small-unit operations, low-altitude mountaineering, and infiltration/exfiltration techniques via land, air, and sea, both day and night. Upon successful completion of training he is authorized to wear the Ranger Tab.

The Ranger Creed

Recognizing that I volunteered as a Ranger, fully knowing the hazards of my chosen profession, I will always endeavor to uphold the prestige, honor, and high esprit de corps of my Ranger Regiment.

Acknowledging the fact that a Ranger is a more elite soldier who arrives at the cutting edge of battle by land, sea, or air, I accept the fact that as a Ranger my country expects me to move further, faster and fight harder than any other soldier.

Never shall I fail my commrades. I will always keep myself mentally alert, physically strong, and morally straight and I will shoulder more than my share of the task whatever it may be. One hundred-percent and then some.

Gallantly will I show the world that I am a specially selected and well trained soldier. My courtesy to superior officers, neatness of dress, and care of equipment shall set the example for others to follow.

Energetically will I meet the enemies of my country. I shall defeat them on the field of battle for I am better trained and will fight with all my might. Surrender is not a Ranger word. I will never leave a fallen comrade to fall into the hands of the enemy and under no circumstances will I ever embarrass my country.

Readily will I display the intestinal fortitude required to fight onto the Ranger objective and complete the mission, though I be the lone survivor.

The M240B machine gun has replaced the aging M60 in the Ranger armory. It uses the same 7.62mm ammunition as the older M60 and is effective in laying down suppressive fire when engaging the enemy. *U.S. Army Special Operations Command*

The M224 60mm lightweight company mortar system is ideally suited to Ranger operations. *U.S. Army Special Operations Command*

A member of the 75th Ranger Regiment sets up the 60mm mortar. *U.S. Army Special Operations Command*

A Ranger checks his target prior to shouldering his M3 Carl Gustav rifle. The M3 is an antitank weapon system firing a variety of 84mm ammunition. Originally fielded to the Rangers in 1990, the program has grown to include SEALs. Depending on ammunition type, the effective range varies from 200 to 1,300 meters. Manufactured by Bofors of Sweden, the rifle weighs approximately 25 pounds and is 42 inches long. *U.S. Army Special Operations Command*

Vietnam

The 75th Ranger Regiment is linked directly and historically to the 75th Infantry companies that were active in Vietnam. Units of the 75th Infantry were converted to Long Range Patrol units. Volunteers to these units were assigned to various Ranger companies where training was often a combat mission. Not until a volunteer had a series of combat missions under his belt would he be accepted by his peers; at this time, he would be allowed to wear the black beret and the scroll shoulder insignia of the Ranger company.

Methods of operations for the Long Range Patrols were varied, but the helicopter was the primary means for insertion and exfiltration in enemy rear areas. Other methods included foot, wheeled, tracked vehicle, airboats, navy swift boats, and stay-behind missions, which called for Rangers to remain in place while a larger infantry unit withdrew. General missions consisted of locating the enemy bases and lines of communication. Special missions included wiretap, prisoner snatch, platoon- and company-sized raid missions, and bomb damage assessment following B-52 Arc-Light missions.

Grenada

During Operation Urgent Fury, the Rangers were deployed to Grenada on 25 October 1983. Their mission was to protect American medical students and restore democracy to the island. During this operation, members of the 1st and 2nd Ranger Battalions conducted an audacious low-level parachute assault (500 feet), seizing the airfield at Point Salinas, rescued American citizens at the medical campus, and conducted air assault operations.

Panama

The entire Ranger regiment participated in Operation Just Cause in Panama. Rangers spearheaded the action by conducting two important operations. The 1st Battalion conducted a parachute assault into Omar Torrijos International Airport and Tocumen Military Airfield, to neutralize the Panamanian Defense Forces (PDF), and secured airfields for follow-on forces—in this case, members of the 82d Airborne Division. The 2nd and 3rd Ranger Battalions carried out a parachute assault onto the airfield at Rio Hato, neutralizing the PDF and seizing General Manuel Noriega's beach house.

Iraq

Elements of the 75th Ranger Regiment deployed to Saudi Arabia in February 1991 in support of Operation Desert Storm. The Rangers conducted raids and provided a quick reaction force in cooperation with Allied forces; there were no Ranger casualties.

In Operation Iraqi Freedom, U.S. Army Rangers from the 75th Ranger Regiment, supported by the paratroopers of the 173rd Airborne Brigade, performed a low-level parachute drop using C-17 Globemaster transport aircraft.

The RSOV measures 173.8 inches long, 70.5 inches wide, and 76 inches high (without gun mount). It has a ground clearance of 10 inches. Fully loaded, the vehicle weighs 7,734 pounds. The RSOV is powered by a four-cylinder turbocharged diesel engine. It has a range of 200 miles, which can be extended by 50 miles per extra 5-gallon fuel can.

These forces secured the airfield in Bashur, Northern Iraq. Along with the Rangers were Air Force Special Operations Command assets, who provided air traffic control. This airborne assault was heralded as the most intricate combat airborne operation since World War II. A makeshift sign now identifies the airfield as "Bush International Airport."

The Rangers also performed airfield seizure of two major airfields, H-2 in western Iraq and H-3 in the southwest. Besides seizing the airfields, the Rangers also assaulted the Baath Party headquarters in western Iraq. This premier light infantry strike force also attacked command and control sites throughout Iraq, cutting off the communications network between the regime and its forces.

Operation Enduring Freedom

Members of the 75th Ranger Regiment were instrumental in seizing the Hadithah dam and preventing it from being destroyed by the Iraqi army. Such actions would have caused flooding of the Euphrates River, which leads south toward Baghdad. The more immediate threat of flooding the area of Karbala might have hindered or trapped certain coalition forces.

The RSOV is air deployable in any of the current air force tactical cargo aircraft and can be internally transported in both MH-47 and MH-53 helicopters.

Somalia

Elements of the 75th Ranger Regiment deployed to Somalia to assist in humanitarian operations by United Nations forces to bring order to a desperately chaotic and starving nation. Their mission was to capture key leaders, to end clan fighting in and around Mogadishu.

On 3 October 1993, members of Task Force Ranger (TFR) conducted a daylight raid on an enemy stronghold deep in militia-held Mogadishu. Delta Force operators were tasked with the capture of two of warlord Aidid's lieutenants. According to intelligence support activity sources, these aides were in the building a block away from the Olympic Hotel. This was in the Bakara area, one of the most dangerous parts of the city.

Helicopters from the 160th SOAR(A) launched from the TFR compound at Mogadishu airport at 1532 hours, with a ground convoy moving out shortly thereafter. Aircraft heading for the target included two MH-6 Little Birds with the lead Delta teams; eight Blackhawks, carrying additional Delta assaulters and members of the 75th Ranger Battalion; a combat search-and-rescue helicopter; and the C&C (command and control) helicopter.

Using rocket-propelled grenades, the Somalis managed to knock down some of the helicopters inserting members of TFR. What started out as a simple assault turned into a ferocious firefight, and TFR would literally have to fight their way out of the city. Although Task Force Ranger had suffered high casualties, had little or no support and dwindling supplies, and faced a force superior in numbers, they held their ground for more than 18 hours, maintained control of the prisoners, and inflicted an estimated 300 killed

and over 700 wounded. The conflict, in which 18 soldiers of Task Force Ranger were killed, including six Rangers, was called the fiercest firefight in Ranger history since the Vietnam war.

Afghanistan

After the terrorist attacks on the United States on September 11, 2001, members of the U.S. military went on high alert. Members of the 75th Ranger Regiment were among the first American soldiers to carry out the wishes of the National Command Authority. Conducting a night parachute insertion as part of Operation Enduring Freedom, they assaulted and secured a Taliban compound. Upon completing the mission, they were extracted by helicopters of the 160th SOAR(A) and flown to covert bases inside Pakistan. As America continues to prosecute its war on terrorism and terrorist cells, the Rangers will be on call to swoop down and serve as the talons of the American eagle.

On 19 October 2001, four MC-130 Combat Talons from the Air Force Special Operations Command delivered 199 Rangers from the 3rd Battalion, 75th Ranger Regiment. The Rangers descended onto Objective Rhino, southwest of Kandahar, Afghanistan. Supported by AC-130 Spectre gunships, the Ranger assault force seized the isolated desert landing strip, engaged Taliban combatants, and secured the area as a forward aerial refuel/rearm point for future operations.

Embedded into the task force was an Air Force Special Tactics team that provided vital information on the landing strips' usefulness to aircraft for follow-on forces. This site, later called Camp Rhino, was the jumping-off point for the marines for missions in Afghanistan.

"Good to go!" A Ranger applies camouflage prior to an assault.

While most of Special Operations Forces have a tendency to operate in small numbers, Rangers will normally commit a much larger force to engage the enemy. Members of the 3rd Battalion, 75th Ranger Regiment, perform a "mass tac," or mass tactical parachute over the Egyptian desert. Ranger companies were similarly inserted in the wasteland of Afghanistan during Operation Enduring Freedom. *Defense Visual Information Center*

CHAPTER 5

U.S. Army Special Operations Aviation Regiment (SOAR) (160th Airborne)

Motto: Night Stalkers Don't Quit

Supporting the Army Special Operations Forces with aviation assets is the 160th Special Operations Aviation Regiment (Airborne). The regiment consists of modified OH-6 light observation helicopters, MH-60 Blackhawk utility helicopters, and MH-47 Chinook medium-lift helicopters.

The capabilities of the 160th SOAR have been evolving since the early 1980s. Shortly after the failure of Operation Rice Bowl, the attempted hostage rescue mission in Iran, the army formed a special aviation unit. The unit attracted some of the best aviators in the army and immediately began a concentrated training program in low-level flying and night operations.

Members of the 3rd SFG(A) fast-rope out of the rear of an MH-47. An entire ODA can be inserted within 15 seconds of deploying the rope.

The unit became a stand-alone battalion on 16 October 1981. Designated the 160th Aviation Battalion, the unit was commonly known as Task Force 160 because of the constant attachment and detachment of units to prepare for a wide variety of missions. Its focus on night operations resulted in the nickname "Night Stalkers." On 16 May 1990, the unit was reorganized and designated the 160th Special Operations Aviation Regiment (Airborne).

HISTORY

Army Special Operations aviation assets conduct specialized aviation operations in conjunction with other Special Operations forces. These operations include the use of dedicated aviation assets to:

• Insert, extract, and resupply Special Operations forces
• Conduct armed escort, reconnaissance, surveillance, and electronic warfare in support of SOF missions
• Provide command, control, and communications (C3) for SOF elements
• Provide general support aviation during peacetime and contingency operations. The most frequent mission is clandestine penetration for inserting, extracting, and resupplying SOF by air.

Originally known as Task Force 160, the regiment has evolved, and various unit configurations have occurred. Responding to an increased demand for elite, highly trained Special Operations aviation assets, the regiment activated three battalions and a separate detachment and incorporated one National Guard battalion. Today, as in the past, the 160th Special Operations Aviation Regiment (Airborne) remains ready to defeat any threat.

STRUCTURE

The 160th SOAR(A) is based at Fort Campbell, Kentucky, and consists of four active-duty battalions and one forward-deployed company. Its battalions include the Fort Campbell–based 1/160, which flies the AH-6, MH-6, MH-60K, and MH-60L direct-action penetrator (DAP); the Fort Campbell–based 2/160, which flies the MH-47E; the Fort Campbell–based 4/160 Special Operations Aviation Support battalion; and the Hunter Army Airfield, Savannah, Georgia–based 3/160, which flies the MH-60L and MH-47D. D company of the 160th SOAR (D/160) consists of five MH-60Ls based at Fort Kobbe, Panama.

Although all army aviation units have an inherent capability to support Special Operations, the units of the 160th SOAR(A) have been specifically designated by the

The MH-47E is equipped with an integrated avionics system that allows global communications and navigation. It also includes forward-looking infrared and multi-mode radar for nap-of-the-earth flying in poor visibility and bad weather.

secretary of defense to be prepared, trained, and task-organized for Special Operations mission support. The 160th SOAR(A) organizes, trains, equips, validates, employs, sustains, and maintains air assets for worldwide deployment and assignment to theater CinCs for conducting direct action, special reconnaissance, and other special operations.

A "No Fear" logo greets those who board this MH-47 Special Operations helicopter.

Night Stalker Creed

Service in the 160th is a calling only a few will answer for the mission is constantly demanding and hard. And when the impossible has been accomplished the only reward is another mission that no one else will try. As a member of the Night Stalkers I am a tested volunteer seeking only to safeguard the honor and prestige of my country, by serving the elite Special Operations Soldiers of the United States. I pledge to maintain my body, mind, and equipment in a constant state of readiness for I am a member of the fastest deployable Task Force in the world—ready to move at a moment's notice anytime, anywhere, arriving on target plus or minus 30 seconds.

I guard my unit's mission with secrecy, for my only true ally is the night and the element of surprise. My manner is that of the Special Operations Quiet Professional, secrecy is a way of life. In battle, I eagerly meet the enemy for I volunteered to be up front where the fighting is hard. I fear no foe's ability, nor underestimate his will to fight.

The mission and my precious cargo are my concern. I will never surrender. I will never leave a fallen comrade to fall into the hands of the enemy and under no circumstances will I ever embarrass my country.

Gallantly will I show the world and the elite forces I support that a Night Stalker is a specially selected and well trained soldier. I serve with the memory and pride of those who have gone before me for they loved to fight, fought to win, and would rather die than quit. *Night Stalkers Don't Quit!*

The MH-47 conducts overt and covert infiltrations, exfiltrations, air assault, resupply, and sling operations over a wide range of environmental conditions. With the use of special mission equipment and night-vision devices, the aircrew can operate with pinpoint navigation accuracy in hostile environments, over all types of terrain, at low altitudes, during periods of low visibility and low ambient lighting. Here, an MH-47E deploys a Ranger Special Operations vehicle from its cargo bay. *U.S. Army Special Operations Command*

WEAPONS AND EQUIPMENT

MH-6J Little Bird

The MH-6J is a single-engine, light-utility helicopter similar to the Vietnam-era OH-6 "Loach." Based on the Hughes 500 Defender series, the MH-6J, currently manufactured by MD Helicopters, has been modified with outboard platforms on both sides. This configuration, referred to as the external personnel system, can accommodate six external and two internal seating positions. The helicopter is capable of conducting covert infiltrations, exfiltrations, and combat assaults over varying terrain and weather conditions. It can be rapidly configured for FRIES operations.

The MH-6J is also used for command and control and reconnaissance missions. Its small size allows for rapid deployment in C-130, C-141, C-17, and C-5 transport aircraft. With the addition of special racks, it can insert and extract up to two motorcycles.

FRIES is the fastest method of inserting Special Forces soldiers. Once the helicopter is over the insertion point, the rope is deployed. Even as it is hitting the ground, ODA members are jumping on and sliding down, as easily as a fireman slides down a pole.

A good view of the fast-rope attached to the starboard door of an MH-47. The nylon rope allows SOF teams to insert rapidly from their airborne platform.

Fast-roping is similar to sliding down a pole, only this one is suspended up to 90 feet above the ground. These Special Forces soldiers are wearing heavy rappelling gloves to protect their hands from abrasion and friction burns as they ride the rope to the ground.

With the ODA safely on the ground, the helicopter crew members will either release the ropes or, in a covert operation, retract the rope into the aircraft, leaving no sign that an insertion took place.

AH-6J Light Attack Helicopter
The AH-6J is a highly modified version of the McDonnell Douglas 530 series commercial helicopter. The light-attack aircraft has a single turbine engine and dual flight controls. It is employed primarily in close air support of ground troops, target destruction raids, and armed escort of other aircraft.

MH-60 Blackhawk
The 160th SOAR(A) operates three Blackhawk variants:

• **MH-60K (Blackhawk),** a version of the Sikorsky UH-60 utility helicopter, modified for Special Operations missions. These modifications include aerial refueling capability, sophisticated aircraft survivability equipment, and improved navigation systems, allowing the helicopter to operate in the most austere environments and adverse weather conditions.

• **MH-60L,** whose primary mission is to carry out infiltration, exfiltration, and resupply operations in a variety of environmental conditions. Secondary missions of the MH-60 include external load, combat search and rescue, and medical evacuation. The MH-60 can operate from a fixed base, remote sites, or ships.

• **MH-60L direct action penetrator (DAP),** equipped with assorted weapons systems. Its primary mission is armed escort and fire support, employing precision-guided ordnance in the support of infiltration or exfiltration of small units.

The 160th SOAR(A) operates three models of the Blackhawk. The MH-60K, seen here, is a highly modified twin-engine utility helicopter based on the Sikorsky UH-60 airframe but developed for Special Operations missions.

MH-47

The MH-47's primary mission is overt and covert infiltration, exfiltration, air assault, and resupply of SOF teams. The 160th SOAR(A) currently operates two models: the MH-47D adverse weather cockpit, capable of operating at night during the worst weather conditions, and the MH-47E, nicknamed the "Dark Horse." Like its sister ship, this heavy assault helicopter was designed to support SOF missions.

The MH-47D Chinook is a twin-engine, tandem-rotor, heavy-assault helicopter modified for the 160th SOAR(A). It is equipped with weather avoidance/search radar, an aerial refueling probe for inflight refueling, forward-looking infrared (FLIR), secure communications, and a navigation system It has a fast-rope insertion extraction system for inserting and extracting personnel. It is armed with two M-134 machine guns (port and starboard) and one heavy machine gun on the rear cargo ramp.

The MH-47E is a heavy-assault helicopter based on the CH-47 airframe, designed and built for the Special Operations aviation mission. It has a totally integrated avionics subsystem that combines a redundant avionics architecture with dual mission processors, remote terminal units, and multifunction displays and display generators, to improve combat survivability and mission reliability. It also has an aerial refueling probe for inflight refueling, an external rescue hoist, and two L714 turbine engines with full authority digital electronic control, which provides more power in hot and high environments. Two integral aircraft fuel tanks replace the internal auxiliary fuel tanks commonly carried on the MH-47D, providing 2,068 gallons of fuel with no reduction in cargo capacity.

The MH-47D Chinook is a twin-engine, tandem-rotor, heavy-assault helicopter modified for the 160th SOAR(A). It is armed with two M-134 machine guns (port and starboard) and one heavy machine gun on the rear cargo ramp. *U.S. Army Special Operations Command*

MISSIONS

Task Force 160 received its baptism by fire when helicopters inserted Delta Force operators onto Grenada during Operation Urgent Fury in 1983. Since then, the unit has responded to numerous missions at the request of the National Command Authority. This includes the successful Mount Hope III Operation in June 1988, performed in the most demanding environmental flight conditions imaginable, clearly demonstrating the ability of man and machine to strike deep, accomplish the mission, and return safely. Equipped with MH-47 Chinooks, MH-60 Blackhawks, and Little Birds, the 160th provided a clandestine insertion platform for Special Operations forces in retrieving a Russian MI-24 Hind attack helicopter from Chad.

Night Stalkers participated in Operations Earnest Will and Prime Chance in 1987, where they provided patrol assistance and escort for Kuwaiti oil tankers in the Strait of Hormuz and Persian Gulf region. The aircrews conducted sustained operations and supported a joint military task force of naval vessels and SEALs under extraordinarily difficult and hazardous conditions. Aircrews of the 160th regularly operated 30 feet above the water, at night, using night-vision goggles and forward-looking infrared devices. It was the first successful night-combat engagement that neutralized an enemy threat using these devices.

The MH-6J Little Bird is a single-engine, light utility helicopter based on the Hughes Defender 500 airframe. It has been modified to externally transport up to six combat troops and their equipment.
U.S. Army Special Operations Command

Panama

Night Stalkers were called upon in December 1989 to spearhead Operation Just Cause, the liberation of Panama. Soldiers of the 160th deployed from Fort Campbell during the harshest winter conditions on record into the sweltering darkness of Panama. Night Stalkers conducted successful pre-H-Hour combat airborne and air assaults, striking the first blows to oust a hostile dictator and safeguard American and Panamanian lives.

Their small but agile Little Birds were used in Operation Acid Gambit, which again saw the partnering of the 160th SOAR(A) with operators from Delta Force. The mission was the rescue of a U.S. national, Kurt Muse, who was being held by General Noriega in Modelo Prison.

The Night Stalkers continued to carry out an assortment of tasks in Operation Just Cause, from searching for the elusive dictator to providing fire support for ongoing missions. In the end, the pilots of the 160th shuttled the captured Manuel Noriega from the Papal Nuncio grounds to Howard Air Force Base, where he was transferred to an MC-130 and transported to the United States.

Iraq

In August of 1990, the Iraqi army's irresponsible and irrational destruction of Kuwait was met by the rapid establishment of Special Operations aviation assets in the Southwest Asia theater of operations (because CENTCOM's area of responsibility encompasses this entire area, not just the Middle East.) SOAR's operations showed the 160th's ability to conduct complicated night and sustained-combat operations as a unit against a determined enemy. In Desert Shield and again in Desert Storm, pilots of the 160th SOAR(A) would be instrumental in inserting and extracting U.S. SOF teams.

A Night Stalker MH-60 takes on fuel from a MC-130 Combat Shadow. Mid-air refueling gives the helicopters an extended range for insertion and extraction of SOF units.

The basic MH-6 configuration consists of the external personnel system mounted on each side of the aircraft, for a total of six external and two internal seating positions. The small size of the Little Bird allows it to maneuver in much tighter space than the larger Blackhawk and Chinook helicopters. Here, an MH-6 inserts a team of Rangers at street level. *U.S. Army Special Operations Command*

The *Delta Queen* is a method for retrieving and extracting the team. The team meets up with an MH-47E Chinook of the 160th SOAR(A). The pilot brings his aircraft to a hover, then closer and closer to the water's surface, until it rests on the water. With the rear cargo ramp lowered, the MH-47E begins to take on water. Wave after wave cascades over the ramp, and soon the flight engineers are standing in water over the tops of their boots. As the Zodiac begins to line up with the rear of the chopper, a helicopter crew member holds a red-filtered light to signal the team. The exfiltrating team aims for the ramp and the now-flooded fuselage, guns the engine, and ducks their heads. With a splash and a thud, the team is aboard. As the helicopter lifts off, all the water rushes out the rear cargo ramp, like a waterfall.

Based out of King Khalid International Airport in Saudi Arabia, the Night Stalkers began operations in September 1990. A primary mission assigned to the 160th SOAR(A) was to provide infil/exfil for SOF units. A secondary mission was to be on call to carry out combat search and rescue missions as the need arose.

In February 1991, a Joint Special Operations Task Force arrived in Saudi Arabia. With approximately 400 men, the task force included the 160th SOAR(A) and Delta Force. Their mission was to locate and destroy the Iraqi SCUD missiles and their mobile launchers. Delta operators, working in conjunction with the British 22 SAS in western Iraq, conducted what became known as the "The Great SCUD Hunt."

Inserted by MH-47 helicopters of the 160th SOAR(A), the Delta teams unloaded their fast-attack vehicles and began their mission. Although the vehicles were heavily armed, the most lethal weapon in their inventory was the laser acquisition marker, which could "paint" a target and deliver precision-guided munitions onto the SCUD targets.

The 160th was also instrumental in successfully inserting and extracting a number of Special Forces teams in Iraq prior to H-Hour. This involved flying nap-of-the-earth, sometimes flying so low that on one occasion the tail wheel of an MH-60 hit a sand dune. Undaunted, the pilot just drove on! Using night-vision goggles, the Night Stalkers delivered these teams to their locations with pinpoint accuracy and, with like precision, extracted them when the time came.

As the war on terrorism expanded to other regions of Southeast Asia, the 160th was instrumental in infiltrating and exfiltrating SOF units into and throughout Iraq. In preparation for Operation Iraqi Freedom, the 160th inserted Special Forces Operational Detachment-Alphas, who worked behind the scenes with Kurdish guerrillas to bring pressure on Iraqi army units.

Off to the west, helicopters from SOAR(A) would deliver Rangers who performed airfield seizures. In other undisclosed areas, Delta Force teams hunted for high-ranking members of the Iraqi regime as well as the elusive SCUD missiles.

Throughout the region, 160th assets would be utilized in the largest employment of U.S. Special Operations Forces since the Vietnam war.

Modifications to the MH-60 helicopters flown by the 160th SOAR(A) allow the helicopter to operate in the most austere environments and adverse weather conditions. *Department of Defense*

Somalia

In October 1993, while supporting Task Force Ranger, Night Stalkers engaged an unconventional hostile force directed by warlord Farah Aidid. The soldiers of the 160th entered into an 18-hour firefight of an intensity that had not been encountered since Vietnam. The dedicated efforts exhibited by these soldiers to overcome adversity and rescue comrades once again demonstrated that Night Stalkers don't quit. The courageous response of the Army's only Special Operations aviation unit has successfully deterred threats by enemies, bolstered national morale and prestige, and supported national foreign policy goals.

Afghanistan

As the United States entered the global war on terrorism after the attacks on America on September 11, 2001, the pilots, aircrews, maintenance crews, and aircraft of the 160th SOAR(A) were again called upon to be at the tip of the spear. Within a month of the terrorist attacks on the World Trade Center and the Pentagon, Special Operations Forces were on the ground in Afghanistan. These lead elements of SOF performed various covert and unconventional missions as a prelude to Operation Enduring Freedom.

Delivering these SOF teams, Night Stalkers not only faced attack by Taliban and al-Qaeda forces but also had to deal with the ever-changing weather. Inserting Special Forces teams in the middle of sandstorms and dense fog while flying a mountainous gantlet, the pilots and aircrews of the 160th delivered their charges with pinpoint precision. On some occasions, the crews found themselves in zero visibility, relying completely on the advance avionics of the MH-47E Chinook.

In addition to clandestine insertion and extraction of SOF assets in the vast region of Afghanistan, the 160th was also tasked to support SOF operations in the Philippines. Here the mission was twofold: first, to assist in hunting down terrorist cells; and second, to support training of Philippine army units. These units would then prosecute the war on terrorism by transforming this training into action in the jungles, hunting down the elusive enemy.

Members of the 7th Special Forces Group (Airborne) perform a "rubber duck" insertion from an MH-47E of the 160th SOAR(A). The team's Zodiac raft, with their equipment secured inside, is pushed from the rear of the hovering helicopter. Immediately after the Zodiac has cleared the ramp, the Special Forces team will follow it out. Swimming to the raft, they will load in and continue their insertion to the target area.

Rangers perform a Fast Rope insertion on to a roof top from a MH-60 during a capabilities exercise at Fort Bragg, North Carolina. *USASOC*

CHAPTER 6

U.S. Air Force Special Operations Command (SOC)

Motto: Any Time, Any Place

The Air Force Special Operations Command (AFSOC), with headquarters at Hurlburt Field, Florida, was established 22 May 1990. AFSOC is the air force component of U.S. Special Operations Command, a unified command. AFSOC is committed to continual improvement to provide Air Force Special Operations Forces for worldwide deployment and assignment to regional linked commands.

AFSOC's mission is to provide mobility, surgical firepower, covert tanker support, and Special Tactics teams. These units normally operate in concert with other Special Operations Forces. AFSOC also provides support to foreign governments and their militaries.

High altitude low opening and high altitude high opening are two methods commonly practiced by Special Operations Forces. Members of the Special Tactics Squadrons are proficient at these techniques for clandestine insertion with army or navy Special Operations Forces.

HISTORY

The origins of today's Air Force Special Operations Command can be traced back to the beginning of World War II. Aircrews and aircraft were utilized in clandestine, unconventional, and psychological warfare in both the European and Pacific theaters.

The forerunner of today's Combat Talon was the highly modified, paint-blackened B-24 Liberator bomber. Members of the 801st Bombardment Group, Army Air Corps, known as the "Carpetbaggers," flew these specialized B-24s. Much like their modern counterparts, these crews became proficient in flying low-level, long-range missions in mountainous terrain, in poor weather, and, of course, at night. These planes were instrumental in delivering covert agents, supplies, and psychological warfare leaflets behind enemy lines.

Agents parachuted into enemy territory were members of the Office of Strategic Services (OSS). Known as Jedburgh teams, they generally consisted of three men, who linked up with partisan resistance fighters to organize and conduct guerrilla operations against the Germans, in preparation for Operation Overlord. In early June 1944, six Jedburgh teams parachuted into strategic locations in Brittany and France, where they relayed critical intelligence in preparation for the Allied invasion of Normandy, 6 June 1944: D-Day.

On another occasion, code-named Halyard Mission, Air Corps Special Operations aircrews were tasked with inserting OSS agents into Yugoslavia. In connection with the partisans, these agents arranged for the return of downed aircrews in Europe. Between June and August 1944, these OSS teams, along with help from the partisans, recovered over 400 American and 80 Allied personnel, who were transported out from covert airfields on Air Corps C-47s.

The Pave Low is an excellent platform for inserting SOF teams. An AFSOC Special Tactics team fast-ropes from the rear of an MH-53H. *Defense Visual Information Center*

Night falls, and a Special Operations team prepares to load up on a Pave Low helicopter. The advanced avionics provide the crew with the means to penetrate enemy lines and insert or extract SOF units. *Defense Visual Information Center*

The other half of the AFSOC team works on the ground. Here, an AFSOC combat control team works at the end of the runway as a C-130 Hercules aircraft comes in for a landing during a joint army/air force exercise. *Defense Visual Information Center*

Special Tactics teams are a combination of combat controllers and pararescuemen, or parajumpers, known as PJs. A combat controller is surrounded by the tools of the trade, from pistols and machine guns, to motorcycles and quads. Whatever it takes to carry out the mission will be available to the teams. *Defense Visual Information Center*

STRUCTURE

The 16th Special Operations Wing is the largest air force unit under the Air Force Special Operations Command, the air force component of the U.S. Special Operations Command. The 16th SOW deploys with specially trained and equipped forces from each service, working as a team to support national security objectives. The 16th SOW manages a fleet of more than 90 aircraft, with a military and civilian work force of nearly 7,000 people. It includes the 4th, 6th, 8th, 9th, 15th, 16th, 20th, and 55th Special Operations Squadrons (SOS).

The 352nd Special Operations Group at RAF Mildenhall, United Kingdom, is the designated air force component for Special Operations Command Europe. Its squadrons are the 7th SOS, which flies the MC-130H Combat Talon II; the 21st SOS, equipped with the MH-53J Pave Low III; the 67th SOS, with the MC-130P Combat Shadow; and the 321st Special Tactics Squadron.

The 353rd Special Operations Group, with headquarters at Kadena Air Base, Japan, is the air force component for Special Operations Command Pacific. The 353rd is composed of three flying squadrons and the 320th Special

Tactics Squadron. The 320th and two of the flying squadrons are located at Kadena Air Base: the 1st Special Operations Squadron (SOS), which flies the MC-130H Combat Talon II, and the 17th SOS, which flies the MC-130P Combat Shadow. The third flying squadron, the 31st SOS, is located at Osan Air Base, Korea, and flies the MH-53J Pave Low III helicopter.

A pair of combat controllers emerges from the water wearing open-circuit SCUBA equipment. The open-circuit system leaves bubbles on the water's surface, whereas the closed-circuit LAR-V leaves none.

Special Tactics Squadrons

Each squadron has three Special Tactics teams, each consisting of 18 enlisted and 2 officers. Half of each team are combat controllers, and the other half are pararescuemen. Teams can also be combat controllers exclusively, their mission being one of direct action.

The team is an integral part of the United States Special Operations Command and its missions. Team members frequently operate with SEALs, Rangers, and Special Forces units in strategic reconnaissance, combat search and rescue, and direct action, such as airfield seizure, to name just a few of their capabilities.

Every member of these teams is a volunteer. These highly motivated, proficient men are capable of being deployed by sea, air, or land, often weighed down with 100 to 150 pounds of equipment to execute their mission. Whether they fast-rope in with a company of Rangers; HALO in with a Special Forces A-Team, or lock out of a submarine with a SEAL platoon, Special Tactics teams add another lethal element to Special Operations Forces.

Operating under AFSOC, Special Tactics Squadrons consist of combat control teams and pararescuemen (PJs). The ratio varies with the mission profile. If the mission is combat search and rescue, the team would be PJ-heavy; whereas if the task is to take down an airfield and hold it, the team would be made up primarily of combat controllers. Each mission profile is unique, and the teams are highly skilled in overcoming, adapting, and improvising to meet their objectives.

Combat Controllers

Combat controllers are proficient in sea-air-land insertion tactics into forward, denied environments. They establish assault zones with an air traffic control capability. Assault zones could be a drop zone for a parachute deployment or a landing zone for heliborne operations, follow-on fixed-wing aircraft, an extraction, or low-level resupply. Combat control teams are also responsible for ground-based fire control of AC-130 Spectregunships.

Besides these capabilities, they provide vital command, control, communications, computers, and intelligence and information (C4I2) capabilities in the forward area of operation and a ground base for fire control for AC-130 gunships. They also establish a recovery zone (to recover troops; the opposite of a landing zone) and are qualified in demolition if they have to remove obstructions and obstacles from the landing zone or drop zone.

Pararescuemen

While combat controllers are busy with their tasks, pararescuemen provide any trauma medical care necessary to stabilize and evacuate injured personnel. They provide triage and medical treatment for follow-on forces and are instructed in the latest medical procedures in combat and trauma medicine. They may also serve on AFSOC aircraft as gunners and/or scanners or participate in combat search-and-rescue operations. To say that these individuals are highly skilled would be an understatement.

TRAINING

Training for Special Tactics Squadron members, called the "pipeline," is a long and arduous journey that takes the prospective combat controller 35 weeks to complete. For pararescuemen the timing is even longer, with the addition of medical training at the Joint Special Operations Medical Training Center at Fort Bragg.

The pipeline begins with a one-week orientation at Lackland Air Force Base, Texas. Here, students spend most of their time in preparation and physical development for subsequent courses. They also learn the history and fundamentals of combat control.

After orientation, they move on to the combat control operator course at Keesler Air Force Base in Mississippi. For the next 15 1/2 weeks, they learn the bread and butter of the combat controller's mission: aircraft recognition and performance, air navigation aids, weather, airport traffic control, flight assistance service, communication procedures, conventional approach control, radar procedures, and air traffic rules.

They spend the next three weeks at Fort Benning and the U.S. Army Airborne School, where they learn the basics of static-line parachuting. This includes ground week, tower week, and jump week, where they make five jumps. Upon completion of the course, they are awarded the Silver Wings of a paratrooper.

Training for STS teams begins at Lackland Air Force Base in San Antonio, where they begin their first step in a year-long training process known as the pipeline. Physical training and conditioning is a must. *Defense Visual Information Center*

The next two and a half weeks are spent in U.S. Air Force Basic Survival School at Fairchild Air Force Base, Washington. There they learn basic survival techniques, including principles, procedures, and techniques to survive and return home from enemy territory.

The final 13 weeks take place at Combat Control School, Pope Air Force Base, North Carolina for the finishing touches. Instruction includes physical training, small-unit tactics, land navigation, communications, assault zones, demolitions, fire support, and field operations, including parachuting. At the completion of this course, each graduate is awarded the scarlet beret and combat controller flash.

Next is advanced skills training, which takes place from the first duty station at Hurlburt Field for one year. It includes initial familiarization and other advanced-skills schools.

Operating since 1997, initial familiarization acquaints newly assigned or recently transferred pararescuemen and combat controllers with the Special Tactics core mission. Students are introduced to or reacquainted with Special Tactics techniques, such as air-field seizure, combat search and rescue, rigging alternate method-zodiac, and call-for-fire missions for fixed and rotary-wing aircraft close air support. Training is done in classrooms as well as in field exercises.

A pair of pararescue insructors drags a "survivor" through the live-fire obstacle range during an exercise at Kirtland Air Force Base, New Mexico. *Defense Visual Information Center*

These pararescue students must become comfortable in the water, which will save their life and the lives of those they are deployed to rescue. *Defense Visual Information Center*

Upon graduation, combat controllers are awarded the scarlet beret and the Air Force combat control crest, "First There." Pararescuemen are awarded the maroon beret with the pararescue crest, "That Others May Live."

Land navigation is essential to the skills of an STS member. Both PJs and combat controllers become experts in using a map and a compass. They also become familiar with celestial navigation. Although they are issued GPS units and are adept at their use, they must always be able to travel from point to point relying on low-tech alternatives.

Advanced schools include the U.S. Army Combat Divers School in Key West. The combat diver course is four weeks long and teaches students the use of open- and closed-circuit SCUBA equipment, underwater search and infiltration techniques, and long-range underwater compass swims.

Navy underwater egress training is a one-day course at Pensacola Naval Air Station that teaches students how to safely exit an aircraft that has landed in the water. Techniques are carried out in a training device known as the dunker, which simulates a sinking aircraft.

The final advanced school of this phase is the U.S. Army Military Free Fall Parachutist School. This course is five weeks, beginning with training at Fort Bragg and progressing to the Yuma Proving Grounds in Arizona. Students learn high altitude low opening (HALO) and high altitude high opening (HAHO) parachuting techniques. Each student makes a minimum of 30 free-fall parachute jumps, including two day and two night jumps.

WEAPONS AND EQUIPMENT

AC-130U Spectre Gunship

Gunships trace their heritage back to Vietnam: Puff the Magic Dragon, Spooky, Stinger, and finally the moniker that stayed, the Spectre. These names all brought fear to the hearts of the enemy and relief to U.S. troops, both Special Forces and conventional. From the original AC-47, with its multiple miniguns, through today's AC-130 Spectre, the gunship has evolved into a sophisticated, highly technical aircraft capable of turning the night sky into death.

The newest of the Spectre gunships, the AC-130U, is the flagship of the air commando skies. Built with Special Operations in mind, at a cost of $72 million each, its primary mission is to deliver precision firepower in support

Nose art of a Vietnam-era AC-47 gunship. The air commando crest is still in use today, and AFSOC carries on in the proud heritage of "Any Time, Any Place." The ghost carrying the lightning bolt was symbolic of the gunships. The symbol and the name "Spooky" are used today by the 4th Special Operations Squadron, who fly AFSOC's AC-130U Spectre gunships.

The flagship of the U.S. Air Force Special Operations Command is the AC130U Spectre gunship, seen here in operations with the 4th Special Operations Squadron at Hurlburt Field.

of close air support for Special Operations and conventional ground forces. It carries a crew of 13 and is armed with a 25mm machine cannon, a 40mm Bofors cannon, and a 105mm howitzer. The Spectre can provide accurate fire support with limited collateral damage and can remain on station for extended periods. These activities are primarily performed in darkness.

During Operation Restore Democracy in Haiti, Lieutenant Colonel Tim Schaffer of the 4th Special Operations Squadron reported that AFSOC put the Spectres on station, even though there was no hostile activity. "It gave the troops on the ground peace of mind to hear the drone of those engines overhead, just in case."

Spectre gunners prepare the 105mm howitzer for firing. With a maximum effective range of over six miles, the weapon is extremely effective in engaging the enemy with deadly accuracy. The gunship's weapons are aimed in the aircraft's battle management center. Here, the fire control officer, electronic warfare officer, and enlisted crew members will monitor all-light-level television, thermal imagers, and surveillance and targeting devices. The fire control officer uses a joystick to pick out targets on the ground; this information is then passed to the aircraft commander.

An up-close-and-personal view of the GAU-12 25mm Equalizer chain cannon. The GAU-12 is a six-barrel Gatling gun. Firing high-explosive incendiary ammunition, it is highly effective against light armored vehicles. The GAU-12 is an upgrade from the 20mm gun and is traversable, allowing the gunship to track and attack two targets simultaneously.

MC-130P Combat Shadow

The Combat Shadow extends the range of Special Operations helicopters by providing air refueling. Operations are conducted primarily in formation, at night, and at low level, to reduce the probability of visual acquisition and intercept by airborne threats. This is carried out in clandestine or low-visibility, low-level missions into politically sensitive or hostile territory.

The secondary mission of the Combat Shadow includes delivery of Special Operations Forces. Small teams, assorted gear, Zodiacs, and combat rubber raiding craft are a few of the specialized items the aircraft and its crew convey. The Shadow is a visual flight rule aircraft, used when the pilots can see the ground. Penetrations often use radar.

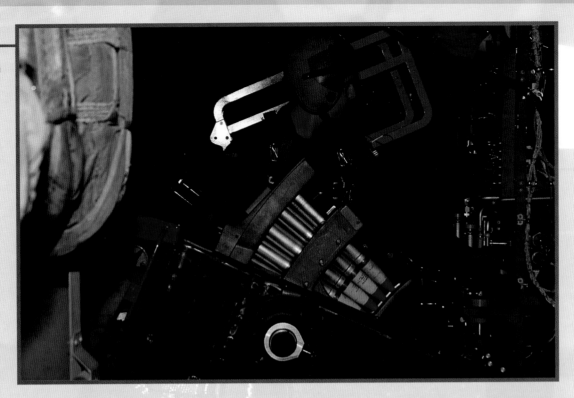

A gunner loads ammunition into and prepares to fire the Bofors 40mm cannon. The 40mm ammo comes in stacks of four per pack and can be continuously fed into the weapon during firing.

An MC-130P Combat Shadow serves as a midair refueling platform for SOF helicopters. It can also serve as an insertion platform and resupply aircraft when necessary.

MC-130E/H Combat Talon

The MC-130E Combat Talon I and the MC-130H Combat Talon II are designed for long-range clandestine or covert delivery of Special Operations forces and equipment. They provide global day, night, and adverse-weather capability.

Combat Talons are equipped with forward-looking infrared, terrain following/terrain-avoidance radar, and specialized aerial delivery equipment. Incorporated into the Talons is a fully integrated inertial navigation, Global

An MC-130H Combat Talon II of the 15th Special Operations Squadron on the tarmac at Hurlburt Field. An air-conditioning unit is attached to the aircraft to keep the avionics cool while running on the ground. Encased in that large nose is the AN/APQ-170 multi-mode radar. Directly beneath can be seen the forward-looking infrared, which allows the Talon to penetrate hostile airspace in the dark.

Positioning System, and high-speed aerial delivery system. The Talons use infrared flight rules, which means the aircraft can be used in heavy ground fog or low cloud cover, when the pilots cannot visually see the ground and must depend on instruments.

EC-130E Rivet Rider Commando Solo

Flown by the 193rd Special Operations Group, the Commando Solo is the only AFSOC asset that is an Air National Guard entity. As the name implies, the Commando Solo works alone. It is capable of conducting day/night overt or covert operations.

Its primary mission is psychological operations, civil affairs broadcast missions, and electronic countermeasures. This is accomplished with standard AM/FM radio, HF/shortwave, TV, and tactical military communications frequencies simultaneously, while loitering outside the lethal range of enemy weapons. The Commando Solo is therefore known as the voice of the quiet professionals.

The crew of the Commando Solo carries out their PsyWar mission both day and night, operating at maximum altitudes to achieve maximum transmission into the area of operation. Typical mission parameters find the EC-130E in a single-ship pattern circling the target audience, whether military or civilian.

MH-53J Pave Low III E

The mission of the MH-53J is to carry out low-level, long-range, undetected ingress into denied or hostile areas. This is accomplished day or night, even under the worst weather conditions, to infiltrate, exfiltrate, and resupply Special Operations forces.

The EC-130 is capable not only of jamming enemy signals and communications but also of pinpointing an enemy's attempt to jam communications. Once located, this information can be passed to the appropriate chain, and the electronic threat can be neutralized. An alternate option would allow an enemy force to communicate and intercept their communications. *Air Force Special Operations Command*

Like its predecessor, the Sikorsky HH-53 Jolly Green Giant of the Vietnam era, the MH-53J Pave Low III Enhanced is the Air Force Special Operations Command's main helicopter. Unlike its predecessor, it has been modified and augmented with state-of-the-art technology that the Jolly pilots would have killed for in their day.

The Pave Low is the largest and most powerful helicopter in the U.S. Air Force inventory and the most technologically advanced helicopter in the world. Equipped with forward-looking infrared, inertial Global Positioning System, Doppler navigation systems, terrain following/terrain-avoidance radar, and integrated

advanced avionics, it can achieve precise, low-level, long-range penetration into denied areas, day or night, in adverse weather and over hazardous terrain without detection.

CV-22 Osprey

The Osprey is a tiltrotor vertical-lift aircraft, which means it takes off like a helicopter and flies like a conventional airplane. However, there is nothing conventional about the Osprey.

The CV-22 is fitted with a refueling probe to facilitate mid-air refueling. The AFSOC Osprey has a modern suite of electronics, like those installed in other AFSOC aircraft, including multimode terrain-avoidance/terrain-following radar. To deal with Special Operations, it has enhanced electronic warfare equipment for increased battlefield awareness: more than 2 1/2 times the volume of flares and chaff, radar jamming gear, and improved integration of defensive counter-measures. For combat search and rescue, it has an internally mounted rescue hoist and a crew door on the starboard side.

An MH53M Pave Low helicopter of the 20th Special Operations Squadron, the Green Hornets, on the tarmac at Hurlburt Field, home of the Air Force Special Operations Command (AFSOC). The origin of this helicopter was the Sikorsky HH3, the "Jolly Green Giant" of the Vietnam era. In addition to its modern electronic wizardry, the helicopter is fitted with two M-134 7.62 miniguns and an M2 .50-caliber machine gun, giving this Hornet a definite sting.

The pilot of this Pave Low is wearing his night-vision goggles in the down position. Special Operations missions are predominantly executed under cover of darkness. This pilot is from the 20th Special Operations Squadron, the Green Hornets.

The pilot or aircraft commander sits in the cockpit of an MH-53M. The commander, copilot, and flight engineer work as a team in an area smaller than some restaurant booths. The Pave Low actually has two pilots. One is designated the aircraft commander and normally sits on the starboard side, although he may choose to sit in the port seat. The second pilot takes the role of copilot.

The starboard gunner of the Pave Low prepares the General Electric M-134 minigun. This 7.62mm minigun is an electrically driven, six-barrel, air-cooled, link-fed Gatling gun. The rate of fire is selectable at 2,000 or 4,000 rounds per minute, with an effective range of 1,000 meters.

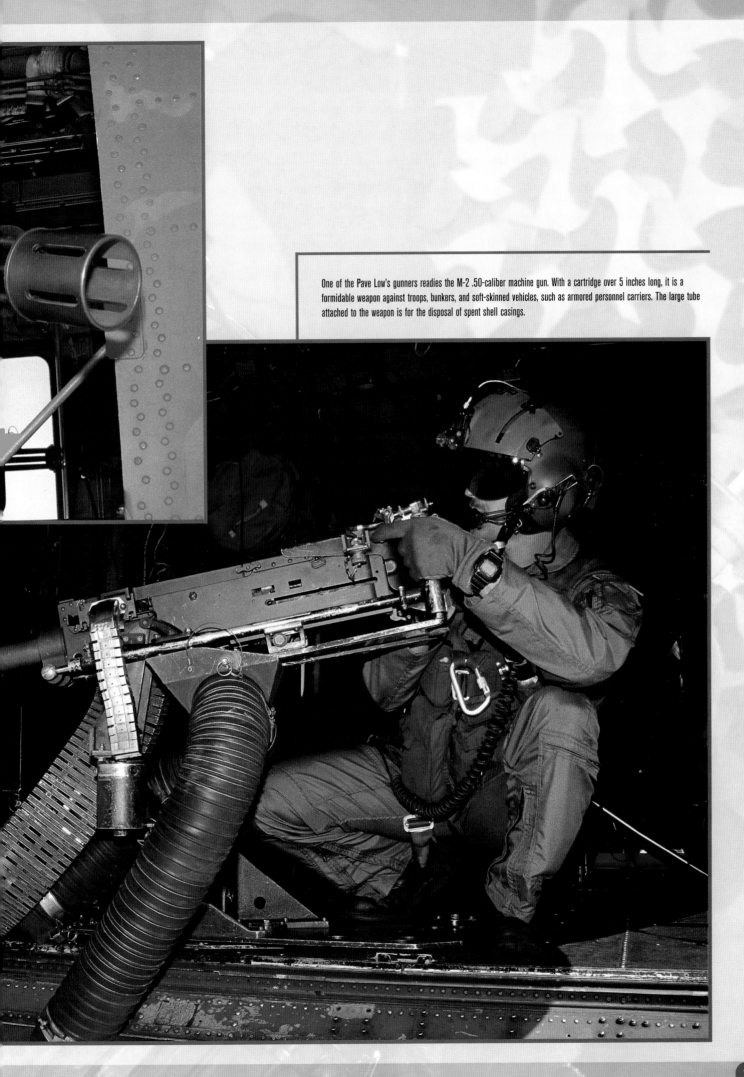

One of the Pave Low's gunners readies the M-2 .50-caliber machine gun. With a cartridge over 5 inches long, it is a formidable weapon against troops, bunkers, and soft-skinned vehicles, such as armored personnel carriers. The large tube attached to the weapon is for the disposal of spent shell casings.

Vietnam

As the war in Vietnam expanded, so did the role of the Air Force Special Operations Forces. General Curtis LeMay responded to this by expanding the 440th CCTS into the Special Air Warfare Center at Eglin AFB in April 1962. The Special Air Warfare Center consisted of the 1st Air Commando Group, the 1st Air Combat Applications Group, and a Combat Support Group. To assist the new organization, the Air Force created a new "counterinsurgency" office specialty code. In an era of nuclear weapons and space missions, this organization had more interest and volunteers than anyone could have imagined.

The Special Air Warfare Center added to its catalogue such aircraft as the O-1 and O-2 observation planes, A-37 and A-1 attack fighters, and C-46, C-119, C-123, and, later, the C-130 cargo aircraft, along with several types of helicopters.

A pair of combat controllers uses a four-wheel-drive quad and motorcycle to assist them in carrying out their mission. Whether performing reconnaissance of an airfield or moving equipment around, these vehicles provide the speed to secure the team's position for follow-on forces to land. *Defense Visual Information Center*

Two STS team members provide security while waiting for the rest of their team to load up on the waiting Pave Low helicopter. *Defense Visual Information Center*

A pararescueman, a member of the Special Tactics team, races down the tarmac, still carrying his rucksack and armed with an M-4 carbine. He will search the runway for foreign objects and debris. Anything that may hamper the follow-on forces from landing will be dealt with expeditiously. He may contact a combat controller to remove it—they are trained to remove such obstacles with explosives if necessary, and pararescuemen are also comfortable with explosives. Shaped charges direct the explosions where the operator wants them to go, to avoid creating holes that would interfere with landing.

Having parachuted into an airfield prior to the follow-on forces, this combat controller prepares to activate the TACAN mounted on the rear of a quad. The TACAN is an omnidirectional navigation beacon that will assist incoming aircraft.

Pararescuemen (PJs) attend to a wounded team member. These PJs are specialists in the treatment of trauma and emergency cases. AFSOC PJs go through the same training as Special Forces medical sergeants at the Joint Special Operations Medical Training Center, Fort Bragg. From simple procedures to the treatment of gunshot wounds, pararescuemen are tops in their field.

In May 1963, the 1st Air Commando Group was redesignated the 1st Air Commando Wing. Operational strength would rise from 2,665 to 3,000, with six squadrons. In the tradition of their predecessors, the Vietnam-era Air Commandos developed techniques that earned their exploits an honored place in Air Force Special Operations heritage.

Grenada

In October 1983, the 23rd Air Force participated with Caribbean forces in successfully rescuing Americans from Grenada. During the seven-day Operation Urgent Fury, centered at Point Salines Airport, the 23rd Air Force Wing furnished MC-130s, AC-130s, and EC-130 aircraft, aircrews, maintenance, and support personnel.

During the Grenada operation, the 1st Special Operation Wing had two missions. MC-130 Combat Talons were tasked with delivering U.S. Army Rangers to Point Salinas. Spectre gunships provided air-to-ground support fire, directed by combat controllers air-dropped in with the Rangers, making an unprecedented combat jump from only 500 feet. Each controller was laden with parachute gear and over 90 pounds of mission-critical equipment.

Upon landing they quickly established a command and control radio net. They carried out air traffic operations for follow-on forces, both at the airport and elsewhere in the country. They also performed as forward air control for Air Force Spectre gunships, Navy fighters, and Army helicopter gunships.

The extreme in low level insertion, going in on foot. If you look under the floppy hats, you can see the secret: the communications headgear used with the inter-team radios—in this case, an AN/PRC-126. These two STS team members are wearing a new type of 3-D camouflage. This camo has leaf patterns attached, to break up any silhouette and allow them to disappear into the surrounding foliage.

Panama

In the 1989 U.S. attack on Panama, Operation Just Cause, pararesuemen and combat controllers participated in operations with the U.S. Army's 75th Rangers at Torrijos Airfield and Rio Hato Air Base. Combat controllers were also attached to U.S. Navy SEAL Team Four, supporting the frogmen who assaulted Patilla Airport to disable General Noriega's personnel jet.

Iraq

Colonel Gary Gray of the 20th Special Operations Squadron was tasked by General Schwarzkopf with kicking off the air war. A flight of four MH-53 Pave Low Green Hornet helicopters led an assault force of army AH-64 Apache helicopters, providing the hammer for the plan called Eager Anvil.

The Pave Lows, equipped with forward-looking infrared, terrain-avoidance radar, Global Positioning System (GPS), and other sophisticated electronics and navigational aids, crossed into Iraq, leading the Apaches through the dark and over the featureless desert to the target areas. Once onsite, the army pilots in their Apaches took out two enemy radar installations simultaneously, with AGM-114 Hellfire laser-guided missiles. Destroying these radar sites opened up a corridor for U.S. and coalition aircraft to begin the air campaign.

Combat controllers provided the air traffic control in Saudi Arabia and virtually ran King Khalid Airport during Desert Shield and Desert Storm. At the beginning of "The Storm," they were with the Special Forces troops that opened the air corridor.

Operation Iraqi Freedom

As in Afghanistan, the personnel of AFSOC would again be called upon to work behind the scenes with other SOF units. Special Tactics teams would parachute in with Army Rangers to secure airfields and establish an airhead for follow-on operations. Pave Low helicopters inserted and extracted American forces for an assortment of clandestine missions.

A member of the 23rd Special Tactics Squadron sights in a target using a laser acquisition marker. When there is no margin for error, you put a Special Operation Forces team on the ground and a fast mover with a smart bomb in the air. Results: one smoking bomb crater. Combat controllers of the Air Force Special Operations Command are specialists in engaging targets with air-to-ground munitions. These men are experts at working with jets or directing close air support fire from other air assets, such as gunships and helicopters.

This combat controller is armed with an M4A1 carbine. Attached to the weapon is an advanced combat optical gunsight four-power scope.

Stealth and secrecy can best be maintained with the help of a sound-suppressed weapon. Here we see the HK Mark 23 Model O SOCOM pistol, with sound suppresser and laser aiming module. Although much longer than the older 1911-style .45-caliber pistols, this handgun is deadly accurate. The suppressor can also be fine-tuned to change the grouping of rounds on target. The laser aiming module has a white light, infrared, and laser sight.

Along with providing air traffic control, Special Tactics teams were instrumental in calling in combat air support missions. On numerous occasions, combat controllers would call in fighters or bombers while "painting" the targets with a laser acquisition marker. The aircraft would then deploy smart bombs, which homed in on the laser. By having an SOF team on the ground lasing the enemy, U.S. and coalition pilots were able to deliver munitions precisely, resulting in less or no collateral damage.

The Commando Solo Rivet Rider also participated in Operation Iraqi Freedom. The following is a sample of a radio message from CENTCOM delivered from the Commando Solo as it flew over Iraq:

> Soldiers of Iraq: Saddam does not care for the military of Iraq. Saddam uses his soldiers as puppets, not for the glory of Iraq, but for his own personal glory. During the Gulf War, Saddam put his own soldiers out in the desert without supplies or support, to stop the coalition forces who had expelled the Iraqi military from their illegal occupation of Kuwait. He also laid land mines to the rear of their positions. Not only did Saddam needlessly put you in harm's way against the coalition forces, he also prevented your safe return.

Somalia

Three sergeants of the 24th Special Tactics Squadron (STS) were with the Rangers in Somalia. It was a textbook example of exploiting the talents of STS members. Combat controllers would call in air fire within meters of their own position. They would literally blow out one wall, then another, and thus were able to escape out of harm's way.

Haiti

While network news crews showed U.S. helicopters settling into a landing zone in Haiti during Operation Restore Democracy, hailing them as "the first Americans to land on Haitian soil," members of the Air Force Special Tactics Squadron had already been on the ground for days, surveying the helicopter landing zone and setting up lighting for the heliborne troopers.

Afghanistan

During Operation Enduring Freedom, AFSOC took an active role in bringing the war to the enemy. Special Tactics teams were embedded with Army Special Forces teams working with the Northern Alliance in Afghanistan. Highly skilled in the art of close air support, combat control teams engaged Taliban and al-Qaeda forces. Whether calling in the fast movers (jets), attack helicopters, or AC-130 Spectre gunships, these air commandos brought a new dimension of warfare to this ancient land. There is no deadlier, more accurate, or more lethal combination in the SOF arsenal than a combat controller on the ground and an AC-130 gunship orbiting overhead.

As early as October 2001, Special Tactics teams had infiltrated Afghanistan, embedded with Army Special Forces Operational Detachment-Alpha. The mission of the 12-man ODA was to organize the Northern Alliance forces into a formidable force against the terrorists. The mission of the AFSOC STS team was to provide necessary support to the Special Forces and Northern Alliance soldiers against Taliban and al-Qaeda targets.

Using spotting scopes and high-powered binoculars with range-finding reticles, combat controllers would identify enemy positions. Then, using GPS units and maps, they would plot the target and call for an air strike. On one occasion, a combat control "painted" a target, and a navy F-18 Hornet carrying precision-guided bombs sent the ordnance right into the front door of an enemy bunker. In addition to the fighters, combat controllers also called in heavy bombers, such as the B-52 Stratofortress.

Gunships from Hurlburt Field's Special Operations Wing brought constant and devastating power down on the enemy. From attacking al-Qaeda compounds to destroying Taliban convoys, these precision weapons platforms brought a new meaning to "death from above."

In addition to the gunships, MC-130H Combat Talons inserted Army Rangers at Objective Rhino in Northern Iraq. The MC-130P Combat Shadow was on station for refueling the many SOF helicopters, AFSOC and army alike, along with the EC-130E Commando Solo, AFSOC's PsyWar aircraft.

Besides operating in Afghanistan, AFSOC members were also deployed to the Philippines with other SOF units, to participate in America's global war on terrorism.

"Call for fire." An STS team leader calls in coordinates to the AC-130U Spectre gunship on station using an AN/PRC-117, while his teammate provides cover with a CAR-15—a carbine version of the M16, predecessor to the M4. A Special Tactics team member on the ground and a Spectre overhead is a lethal combination.

CHAPTER 7

Counterterrorist and Other Elite Forces

Special Mission Units

The Department of Defense has acknowledged the formation and maintenance of selected Special Mission units (SMUs) specifically organized to conduct highly classified and usually compartmented Special Operations missions. A primary mission includes covert action teams to combat terrorism and counterterrorist use of weapons of mass destruction. These SMUs are routinely under the direct supervision of the highest command levels, usually the National Command Authority. They are specially manned, equipped, and trained to deal with an assortment of international threats.

The SMUs are under the control of the Joint Special Operations Command at Fort Bragg. It is generally understood that the SMUs include the army's Combat Applications Group (CAG) and the Naval Special Warfare Development Group (DEVGRU). The army's 75th Ranger Regiment and the 160th Special Operations Regiment can be assigned as needed to augment the SMU, whose tactics, techniques, procedures, equipment, and personnel remain classified.

Without a doubt, the marines produce some of the best riflemen in the world. Here, a Force Recon Marine has the extra skill of scout/sniper. Armed with an M-40 sniper rifle, he is trained to engage an enemy out to 1,000 meters. The snipers' motto: "One shot. One kill."

167

These units are prepared and trained to execute various Special Operations under covert or clandestine circumstances while maintaining absolute minimum individual and organizational visibility during day-to-day operations. If called into action, they operate under two classified contingency plans that address counterterrorism and counterproliferation. The SMUs are also understood to have been planning to counter any use of weapons of mass destruction by Iraq, including deploying Joint Special Operations Command forces to the region.

DELTA FORCE

Delta Force is officially designated the 1st Special Forces Operational Detachment-Delta (SFOD-D). The unit has a cover name: Combat Applications Group, or CAG. The official comment from SOCOM on CAG states, "Effective 1 October 1991, the U.S. Army Combat Applications Group (Airborne) was activated as a subordinate element of the U.S. Army Special Operations Command (USASOC). Formed during the restructuring of Army special operations assets, the CAG (Abn) tests special operations methods, equipment, tactics, and combined arms interoperability with a focus of the development of doctrine beyond the year 2000."

The U.S. Army's 1st Special Forces Operational Detachment-Delta is one of two of the U.S. government's principal units tasked with counterterrorist operations outside the United States (the other being Naval Special Warfare Development Group). Delta Force was created by U.S. Army Colonel Charles Beckwith in 1977, in direct response to numerous well-publicized terrorist incidents that occurred in the 1970s. From its beginnings, Delta was heavily influenced by the British Special Air Service (SAS), a philosophical result of Col. Beckwith's year-long (1962–63) exchange tour with that unit.

Accordingly, it is today organized into three operating squadrons, all of which (A, B, and C) are subdivided into small groups known as troops. It is rumored that each troop, as is the case with the SAS, specializes in HALO, SCUBA, or other skill groups. These troops can each be further divided into smaller units as needed, to fit mission requirements. Delta also maintains support units, which handle selection and training, logistics, finance, and the unit's medical requirements. Within this grouping is a little-known but vital technical unit, responsible for covert eavesdropping equipment used in hostage rescues and similar situations.

These skills are enhanced by the unit's participation in an ongoing exchange and training programs with foreign counterterrorist units, including (as might be expected) Britain's 22 SAS, France's GIGN, Germany's GSG-9, Israel's Sayeret Matkal/Unit 269, and Australia's own Special Air Service Regiment. Such close cooperation with other groups provides innumerable benefits, including exchanges of new tactics and equipment as well as enhancing relations that might prove useful in later real-world operations.

The vast majority of the unit operatives come from the United States' elite Ranger battalions and Special Forces groups, but candidates are drawn from all branches of the army, including the Army Reserve and National Guard. Those initially selected are usually chosen in one of three ways. The first is in response to advertisements posted at army bases across the country. The second is word-of-mouth or personal recommendation from sources whose opinions are important to Delta screeners. Finally, on occasion, the unit requires the skills of individuals who might not fall into one of the first two categories. If Delta's commanders feel that an individual would make a valuable addition to the team (for example, someone who speaks an obscure language or possesses hard-to-come-by technical skills), a representative from Delta will be dispatched specifically to interview that person.

NAVAL SPECIAL WARFARE DEVELOPMENT GROUP [NSWDG]

The NSWDG, more commonly called DEVGRU, is the maritime version of the Army Combat Applications Group (CAG), which is better known as Delta Force. DEVGRU was created the mid-1990s after the declared disbanding of SEAL Team Six. The Navy's official comments on the unit state its mission is to create, test, and evaluate new tactics, weapons, and equipment for the NSW community. Based in Dam Neck, Virginia, DEVGRU has approximately 400 operators and support personnel which are divided into four combat teams and one training team. DEVGRU is responsible for U.S. counterterrorist operations in the maritime environment.

Members of DEVGRU are constantly training throughout the United States as well as in conjunction with our allies throughout the world. Through the use of exchange programs and joint trainings exercises and missions, these highly skilled CT operators may find themselves in the company of the British Special Boat Squadron (SBS) units, Australian Special Air Service (SAS) teams, or other highly covert special operations operators among other allies forces. There training is intense with the maxim, "The more you sweat in peace; the less you'll bleed in war."

U.S. MARINE CORPS
FORCE RECONNAISSANCE

The Force Reconnaissance companies of the U.S. Marines are not part of SOCOM and are not considered Special Operations Forces. This was more a political than a strategic decision. Marine commanders were concerned that if Force Reconnaissance units were absorbed into the newly created SOCOM organization, they would no longer be assets to the Corps. Thus, while the marines receive the same training as other SOF units, they are consider Special Operations Capable.

The Marine Expeditionary Unit (Special Operations Capable) MEU(SOC) is the smaller and more visible type of Marine Air-Ground Task Force concept, containing an average of 1,500 to 3,000 marines. It is equipped with supplies to sustain itself for up to 30 days and can provide a quick-reaction force.

There are currently seven MEU(SOC)s in the U.S. Marine Corps. The 22nd, 24th, and 26th are based on the East Coast, at Camp Lejeune, North Carolina; the 11th, 13th, and 15th are based on the West Coast, out of Camp Pendleton, California; and the 31st is in Okinawa, Japan. At any given time, two or more of these units are forward deployed. Regardless of the task, the MEU(SOC) stands ready to respond and can have forces on-site within six hours of getting the "go" call.

The Marine Corps is not part of SOCOM and thus is not referred to as Special Operations Forces. However, members of the Marines' Force Reconnaissance companies do receive the same training as SOCOM SOF units and are therefore considered Special Operations capable. This Force Recon Marine is wearing the newly issued camouflage uniform unique to the Corps.

The primary mission of Force Recon teams is to provide deep penetration reconnaissance behind enemy lines for the commander of the marine expeditionary unit. These units may be inserted via parachute, submarine, or boots to carry out their missions.

It may not be the fastest way in, but it is the stealthiest. A team of Force Recon Marines moves through a swamp, leaving no trace of their insertion.

The Marine Expeditionary Unit (Special Operations Capable) is groomed for the contingency battles of the future. Based on naval vessels, the forward-deployed MEU(SOC) is uniquely organized to provide the naval or joint force commander with an expeditionary force that is inherently balanced, sustainable, flexible, responsive, and expandable.

Commanded by a colonel, with a combat strength of approximately 2,000 marines and sailors, it is a small yet formidable force-in-readiness. Normally embarked aboard three ships of an Amphibious Ready Group, it is task-organized to accomplish a broad range of mission requirements. MEU(SOC)s are most frequently deployed within the Pacific, Atlantic, and Indian Oceans, but are available for deployment to any region around the world. With the decline of American bases abroad, MEU(SOC) is possibly the only U.S. force available that can respond to any worldwide crisis in as little as six hours. This availability and readiness has earned the marines of the MEU(SOC) the mark of distinction as "America's 911 Force."

Force Reconnaissance (FORECON) is employed as an asset to the MEU(SOC); it is in direct support of the MEU's operational directives and thereby direct support of the Marine Expeditionary Forces commander. The FORECON mission is to conduct amphibious reconnaissance, surveillance, and direct action.

The Force Reconnaissance Marines are the eyes and ears of the MEU commander. Although Force Recon is a company, it conducts operations as a battalion. Each company has six operational platoons. The operational platoons are staffed with a platoon headquarters consisting of a commander (captain), sergeant (a staff or gunnery sergeant), radio operator (normally a staff or gunnery sergeant), a navy special amphibious reconnaissance corpsman, and a platoon equipment NCO (rigger/armorer).

Each operational platoon is comprised of three six-man teams. The team's table of organization represents functionality based on real-world needs, such as new surveillance and communications equipment. While the new digital communications gear coming online (cameras, computers, etc.) is lighter, stronger, and more efficient than previous gear, there is more of it. A six-man team has enough team members to provide adequate rest while preserving security. Also important is what actions the team has to take should they incur a casualty. The six-man team can double up gear if necessary, whereas a four-man team might have to cache some of its equipment to evacuate a wounded teammate.

In June 2003, a special Marine Corps detachment was created that placed a select group of marines under SOCOM. This detachment, referred to as Marine Special Operations Command (MARSOC), is in a proof-of-concept phase and is intended for eventual assignment to SOCOM. The MARSOC unit consists of 86 marines: a headquarters element, 30 reconnaissance team members, intelligence experts, and fire support specialists (consisting of three air naval gunfire liaison company marines, bringing back the ANGLICO specialty).

The unit has begun training and will participate in joint training with the SEALs in the fall of 2003. If all goes well and the concept is proven sound, this unique unit will most likely be available for deployment in the spring of 2004.

The Force Recon companies include parachute- and SCUBA-qualified Marines. They may use any method of insertion, whether sea, air, or land. Sound familiar?

When it's necessary to take out a larger target, the marines of Force Recon are more than capable of going high-tech. A team member uses a Special Operations Forces laser acquisition marker employed in close air support. The marine will "paint" the target with a laser beam, allowing a smart bomb to home in on the objective and destroy it.

A large percentage of USACAPOC soldiers are from reserve components. Located in 26 states and the District of Columbia, USACAPOC(A) (i.e., airborne) units support theater commanders in meeting their global commitments. USACAPOC(A) soldiers have played a significant role in recent humanitarian missions. They assisted victims of Hurricane Andrew in Florida, coordinated refugee operations for Cubans and Haitians in Cuba, and were among the first soldiers sent to Somalia and Haiti.

The command has one active-duty psychological operations unit, the 4th Psychological Operations Group (Airborne), with six battalions; and one active-duty civil affairs unit, the 96th Civil Affairs Battalion (Airborne), with six companies. Both units are located at Fort Bragg.

Army PSYOP equipment is instrumental in developing and disseminating PSYOP products. Unique equipment assets include 10-kilowatt and 50-kilowatt TV and radio broadcast transmitters, print systems, loudspeakers, and mobile audiovisual vans.
U.S. Army Special Operations Command

Civil affairs soldiers are the field commander's link to the civil authorities in his area of operations. With specialists in every area of the government, they can assist a host government meet its people's needs and maintain a stable and viable civil administration. Since the majority of civil affairs forces are in the reserve component, these soldiers bring to the Army finely honed skills practiced daily in the civilian sector, as judges, physicians, bankers, health inspectors, fire chiefs, and so on.

Psychological operations soldiers use persuasion to influence perceptions and encourage desired behavior. The cornerstone of PSYOP is truth, credibly presented to convince a given audience to cease resistance or take actions favorable to friendly forces. During Desert Storm, the effective use of PSYOP was a combat multiplier that directly contributed to the surrender of thousands of Iraqi soldiers.

U.S. Army PSYOP forces plan and execute the Joint Force Commanders' PSYOP activities at the strategic, operational, and tactical levels; support all Special Operations missions; and conduct PSYOP in support of consolidation missions. Specially trained units support enemy prisoner of war missions.

Psychological operations units also have soldiers with unique skills. These soldiers are communicators who provide the commander with the ability to communicate information to large audiences via radio, television, leaflets, and loudspeakers. The PSYOP soldier's language skills, regional orientation, and knowledge of communications media provide a means of delivering critical information to host-nation audiences.

Civil affairs and PSYOP specialists have been an integral part of peacekeeping operations in Bosnia and Kosovo and are among the most frequently deployed soldiers in the army today. The unique training, experience, and abilities of USACAPOC(A)'s soldiers make them an ideal asset in dealing with national priorities.

Antiterrorism: Defensive measures used to reduce the vulnerability of individuals and property to terrorism.

C4I: Command, Control, Communications, Computers, and Intelligence.

Clandestine operation: Activities sponsored or conducted by governmental departments or agencies so as to assure secrecy or concealment. (It differs from covert operations in that emphasis is placed on concealment of the operation rather than on concealment of the identity of the sponsor.) In Special Operations, an activity may be both covert and clandestine and may focus equally on operational considerations and intelligence-related activities.

Close air support (CAS): Air action against hostile targets that are in close proximity to friendly forces and that require detailed integration of each air mission with the fire and movement of those forces.

Counterproliferation: Activities taken to counter the spread of dangerous military capabilities, allied technologies, and/or knowhow, especially weapons of mass destruction and ballistic missile delivery systems.

Covert operations: Operations planned and executed to conceal the identity of, or permit plausible denial by, the sponsor.

Crisis: An incident or situation involving a threat to the United States, its territories, citizens, military forces and possessions, or vital interests that develops rapidly and creates a condition of such diplomatic, economic, political, or military importance that commitment of U.S. military forces and resources is contemplated to achieve national objectives.

Counterterrorism: Offensive measures taken to prevent, deter, and respond to terrorism.

Direct action mission: An overt, covert, clandestine, or low-visibility mission conducted primarily by a sponsoring power's Special Operations forces in hostile or denied areas.

Exfiltration (exfil): The removal of personnel or units from areas under enemy control.

Humanitarian assistance: Assistance provided by Department of Defense forces, as directed by appropriate authority, in the aftermath of natural or man-made disasters, to help reduce conditions that present a serious threat to life and property. Assistance provided by U.S. forces is limited in scope and duration and is designed to supplement efforts of civilian authorities that have primary responsibility for providing such assistance.

Infiltration (infil): Movement into or through an area or territory occupied by either friendly or enemy troops or organizations. Movement is made either by small groups or individuals, at extended or irregular intervals. When used in connection with the enemy, it implies that contact is avoided.

Internal defense: The full range of measure taken by a government to free and protect its society from subversion, lawlessness, and insurgency.

Lasing: Projecting a laser beam onto a target for laser-guided munitions or smart bombs. Also referred to as "painting" a target.

Low-intensity conflict: A political-military confrontation between contending states or groups below conventional war and above routine, peaceful competition. It frequently involves protracted struggles of competing principles and ideologies. Low-intensity conflict ranges from subversion to the use of armed force. It is waged by a combination of means, employing political, economic, informational, and military instruments. Low-intensity conflicts are often localized, generally in the third world, but contain regional and global security implications.

Psychological operations: Planned operations to convey selected information and indicators to foreign audiences to influence their emotions, motives, objective reasoning, and ultimately the behavior of foreign governments, organizations, groups, and individuals.

Special reconnaissance: Reconnaissance and surveillance conducted by Special Operations Forces to obtain or verify, by visual observation or other collection methods, information concerning the capabilities, intentions, and activities of an actual or potential enemy or to secure data concerning the meteorological, hydrographic, or geographical characteristics of a particular area.

ACRONYMS

AFSOC	Air Force Special Operations Command
ARSOC	Army Special Operations Command
AT	antiterrorism
BDA	bomb damage assessment
BUD/S	basic underwater demolition/SEAL
CA	civil affairs
CAS	close air support
CBT	combating terrorism
CP	counterproliferation of weapons of mass destruction
CQB	close-quarter battle
CRRC	combat rubber raiding craft
CSAR	combat search and rescue
CT	counterterrorism
DA	direct action
DOD	Department of Defense
DZ	drop zone
FAV	fast attack vehicle
FID	foreign internal defense
FOB	forward operation base
FRIES	fast-rope insertion/extraction system
GPS	Global Positioning System
HA	humanitarian assistance
HAHO	high altitude high opening
HALO	high altitude low opening
HE	high explosive
IO	information operations
JCS	Joint Chiefs of Staff
JSOC	Joint Special Operations Command
LBE	load-bearing equipment
LZ	landing zone
MOUT	military operations urban terrain
NOD	night optical device

NSW	naval special warfare
NVG	night-vision goggles
ODA	Operational Detachment-Alpha
OPCON/M	operational control/command
OPSEC	operational security
PSYOP	psychological operations
PSYWAR	pyschological warfare
PZ	pickup zone
SAR	search and rescue
SAS	Special Air Service (U.K. or Australian)
SBS	Special Boat Squadron (U.K.)
SBT	Special Boat Team
SCUBA	self-contained underwater breathing apparatus
SDV	SEAL delivery vehicle
SEAL	Sea Air Land (U.S. Navy Special Operations Forces)
SF	Special Forces (U.S. Army)
SOAR(A)	Special Operations Aviation Regiment (Airborne)
SOCOM	Special Operation Command
SOF	Special Operations Forces
SOFLAM	Special Operations Forces laser acquisition marker
SR	special reconnaissance
STS	Special Tactics Squadron
STT	Special Tactics team
USASFC(A)	U.S. Army Special Forces Command (Airborne)
USASOC	U.S. Army Special Operations Command
UW	unconventional warfare
VBSS	visit, board, search, and seizure
WMD	weapons of mass destruction

INDEX